A CONVERSATIONAL
COMMENTARY
ON THE BOOK OF

EPHESIANS

BY: THOMAS JACKSON, PH.D.

outskirts
press

Thoughts about A Conversational Commentary on the Book of EPHESIANS

Though the bible has been translated into several English, easy-to-read versions, it remains for many a book that is challenging to interpret. In many cases, unless you are a theological academician, everyday people have a difficult time walking away from the bible reading with biblical understanding. In this informative, yet concise, commentary on each of the six chapters of the book of Ephesians, Dr. Thomas Jackson, in an exemplary way, simplifies the ancient text and makes it digestible for both erudite and neophyte, experienced and beginner, biblically literate and biblically illiterate alike. Dr. Jackson's work is both informative and encouraging simultaneously for learning and living with a conversational approach.

- J.K. Hamilton, Author, Speaker
Ministering Evangelist of Christ's church at Mountain View
Dallas, TX

Dr. Thomas Jackson is a student of the Word, who takes a practical and conversational approach to scripture. I found his writings on Ephesians to be easy to read yet engaging. His exegetical insight is visible even though his approach is more like a discussion between two people. He takes advantage of the language idioms of the Greek and Hebrew without the cumbersome and technical citations of tenses, cases and declensions. Yet, their significance is not overlooked. The reader discovers truth in brilliant colors and exciting parallels and symbolism and before finishing, the reader begins to realize that he/she is actually learning and gaining insight into the biblical message. He does all of this without making the reader want to debate the Word, rather finds consolation in the insights shared.

It is a good read and fresh approach to the Ephesian text.

Dr. Loyd Harris, President
School of Religious Studies
Little Rock, AR

Other Publications by Thomas Jackson

Embracing Your Season – Workshop. Five DVD Set.
(Live recording at Ovilla Church of Christ)
Red Oak, TX, 2015.

A Conversational Commentary on the Gospel of JOHN
Outskirts Press, 2014.

Now Is The Time – Workshop. Six DVD Set.
(Live recording at McAlmont Church of Christ)
North Little Rock, AR, 2013.

The ADHD Dialogue – Article.

Low Motives in High Places: A survival strategy for wounded healers
Outskirts Press, 2009.

Man and Woman, As God Has Ordained
Trafford Publishing, 2008

Understanding Schizophrenia – Article.

Understanding African American Behavior in a Euro-American Society – Article.

The Social affects of sons raised by their mothers in the Black Community – Article.

Multiple Personalities or One Personality Expressed in Multiple Ways – Article.

A Daughter's First Romance – Article.

Dedication

To the team of believers from St. Louis, MO, Little Rock, AR, Dayton, OH, and Kingsfisher, OK. Thank you for trusting me enough to travel across the waters and experience the Second Missionary Journey of the Apostle Paul, in the region of Greece. Thank you for your support and encouragement. I personally had a life changing experience during our time in Greece, and to be able to write the first two chapters of this book in modern day Ephesus, was truly a blessing. Let's plan to travel together again.

Acknowledgements

Writing this conversational commentary on the Book of EPHESIANS has a special place in my heart, specifically, being able to write the first two chapters of this book in modern day Ephesus. This experience allowed me to write from a visual perspective. As I wrote, I continued to see, in color, the sites that I visited during my Grecian tour, and now was writing about.

I am truly thankful that as I talked about my experience in Greece and prepared to write this book, that I have a community of supporters and encouragers, who seemed to never tire of listening to my stories or reading my thoughts about the book of Ephesians. My community of supporters and encouragers, include, but not limited to the following people: My children, (**Dillon** & **Kayla**), my wife (**Karla**), the **New Life church family** in St. Louis, MO, **Sandra Blythe** (Editor), **Lee Lewis** (covenant brother), **Jerry Williamson** (great friend), **Delores Chappell** (mother in the gospel), and so many more.

To my **Rose City** church family. Thank you for your confidence and openness to embrace the vision that God has us on as a family. Let us continue to demonstrate the **Power of ONENESS**, as we become **Prayerful in our Hearts, Purposeful in our Actions**, and **Powerful in our Walk**.

Table of Contents

Introduction

It gives me great pleasure and honor to render a word of acknowledgment and praise regarding Dr. Thomas Jackson's, "A Conversational Commentary on the Book of Ephesians." If you have ever heard Dr. Jackson preach, teach or facilitate a workshop, you will find this work to be consistent with his vocabulary, style and manner. In other words, what you have seen is what you will get in this writing. If you have not had that pleasure, what you will get in this writing is what you would see in person (or in one of the many ways he has been recorded and broadcast). In view of this, grant me a preacher's privilege to pursue an alliterative introduction to his commentary, clearly written with skill, knowledge, passion and ability.

From the very first pages of chapter one, you will notice that Jackson's writing is **accessible.** Most of us, as bible students, seek out commentaries to provide us with clarity on just what the Scriptures are saying to us. It is important to remember that we are separated from both the writer and the initial audience by thousands of years, thousands of miles and cultural differences that are unquantifiable. Jackson applies his scholarship as a bridge over that which separates us, to the original author and his intended meaning. As early readers would have well understood colloquialisms, turns of phrases and examples, contemporary ones are used here to help us get the same message. Pay special attention to a description of the Holy Spirit filled apostles, "cutting up so bad, the noise was heard down the street" thereby raising the question of whether they were filled with sweet wine in chapter five. This style of writing brings the word of God right to where it can be reached.

Of course, a commentary is only as good as its ability to be **accurate**. Jackson is well studied and versed in the holy and divinely inspired word of God. It is difficult to get into a conversation with him for more than five minutes that does not include a biblical reference. In the book, he breaks down the word, verse by verse and passage by passage. There is a flow that is consistent with the Scripture and other Scriptural references are brought in to reinforce his point. As Scripture is inerrant, Jackson walks a tight parallel path to ensure that his thoughts do not deviate from the hermeneutical demands of interpretation.

It stands to reason that if any work associated with making the word of God more accessible is also accurate, then it is both my hope and assertion that "A Conversational Commentary on the Book of Ephesians" is **approved**. Two passages of Scripture come to mind as I make this statement. First, "And they continued steadfastly in the apostle's doctrine," Acts 2:42. The mark of any good Christian life, Christian work, Christian teaching or Christian congregation is whether they are found within the framework of the apostle's teaching, which, in and of itself, is no less or different than the teaching of Christ, himself which was received from God, Himself. It is not my goal to equate Jackson with God or his writing with that of the Holy Spirit, but to state that it is consistent with sound doctrine. Secondly, Revelation 22:18-19 provides stark warning to anyone who would add, subtract or make changes to anything "written in the words of the prophecy of this book" can expect grave consequences. Of course, our brother is neither attempting to do this and perhaps not even able, given a strict interpretation of the passage, nevertheless, his overwhelming love for God is expressed in his desire to ensure he is consistent with God's intent as it relates to promulgating the perfect passages.

All said thus far leads me to the conclusion that this commentary is **admirable.** I say this because of the heart of it. When Jackson sits down at his study, communes with his God, meditates on His word, and makes the decision to share with the world a way to even better understand His message for our minds and hearts, it is worthy of commendation. As a fellow author, I can assure you that it is no easy task. Further, the thought processes employed here are both unique and enlightening. Pay close attention to his description of the two Adams in chapter five and the story of redemption expressed by a little boy reacquiring a boat he built in chapter one. Do not be surprised if it elicits a "wow" from you.

Lastly and perhaps most importantly, the work is **applicable.** Though the word of God is entertaining, we do not read it (strictly) to be entertained. Though it is amazing, we do not read it (strictly) to be amazed. Though it is awesome, we do not read it (strictly) to be awed. We read and study the bible to learn God's will for our lives and to be transformed by it. The goal of this commentary is to help us all learn and better understand what thus saith the Lord. As so many of our mothers would say, "when you know better, you do better." Scripture urges us not to be forgetful hearers, but doers of the word. It is much easier to do this when you understand how it applies to life in general and yours specifically.

Beloved reader, it is my hope, trust, and prayer that you will find enlightenment in "A Conversational Commentary on the Book of

Ephesians" by my covenant brother, Dr. Thomas Jackson. I know that you will appreciate the things he has to offer in his book and that it will give you the opportunity to consider the things written by the Apostle Paul in ways that you never have before. If and when that be the case, and it leads you to a closer walk with He who made us, then the goal of this writing will have been met.

May the Lord our God bless and keep you,

Lee E. Lewis, Jr.
Minister
O'Fallon Church of Christ

A Conversational COMMENTARY on the book of Ephesians

A Journey Worth Taking

The Apostle Paul has made a name for himself as a church planter and multiplied his skillset by training other men to do what they had seen him do so well, plant churches through the known world. Approximately 19 churches that we read about in the New Testament were planted by the Apostle Paul or one of his trained colleagues, which spans three missionary journeys, over a ten-year period.

The First Journey

During the first journey the Apostle Paul and Barnabas planted four churches over a two-year period. The churches planted during this journey are: Pisidian Antioch, Iconium, Lystra, and Derbe. The churches make up the region known to us as Galatia. Thus, when Paul writes his letter to the "churches" in Galatia, it is a reference to these four churches.

The Second Journey

During the second journey the Apostle Paul, accompanied by Silas and Timothy, planted an additional four churches within a two-year period. The churches planted during his second journey are: Philippi, Thessalonica, Berea, and Corinth. Over time, Paul will receive questions from the new believers about the faith and they will also inform him regarding the crisis that has occurred in the churches. As a result,

Paul will write a letter to encourage, strengthen, and answer the questions of the believers.

The first letter Paul writes to a church during his second journey is to the Thessalonians. We know this letter as 1 Thessalonians. He then follows up with another letter to the same church, known to us as 2 Thessalonians. Paul will write his letters to Corinth and Philippi during his third journey, but no letter is written to the Berean believers that is recorded in our New Testament canon.

Note: Paul will write his letter to the church in Philippi after he writes his letter to the church in Ephesus; which is one of the eleven churches planted during his third journey and the **focus** of this book.

Third Journey

> "It happened that while Apollos was at Corinth, Paul passed through the upper country and came to Ephesus, and found some disciples." – Acts 19:1 (NASB)

During the third journey the Apostle Paul, accompanied by Epaphras and other co-laborers, planted an additional eleven churches within a three-year period. The churches planted during his third journey are: Ephesus, Troas, and Illyricum by Paul, Laodicea, Colosse, and Hierapolis. The additional co-workers planted churches throughout Asia Minor, including Smyrna, Thyatira, Sardis, Philadelphia, and Pergamum. Paul will later write a letter to the church in Ephesus and Colosse, and both letters are part of our New Testament canon.

Note: Paul also writes letters to the preacher/leader of the church in Colosse and Ephesus. He writes the book of Philemon, who is the leader in Colosse. And, he writes the books of 1 and 2 Timothy, who is the leader in Ephesus.

Laying The Foundation

In Ephesus, two of Paul's co-laborers and tent makers, Aquila and Priscilla, meet a Grecian Jew, from Alexandria, Egypt, named Apollos. Apollos is a well-educated man and skilled in the Old Testament scriptures. He is an eloquent speaker, however, as a believer there is a gap in his understanding of the Lord and Christian baptism; for he only teaches the baptism of John. Aquila and Priscilla, listen to Apollos and take the time to share with him a more informed and accurate account of the gospel and sends him to Corinth to encourage the saints there.

Paul, along with Titus, Gaius, and Timothy arrive in Ephesus and they meet up with three brothers that Paul has sent for and he trains all six men to become church planters in order to spread the community of God throughout all of Asia Minor. The following are the six men that Paul will train as church planters:

1. Titus (from Antioch)
2. Gaius (from Derbe)
3. Timothy (from Lystra)
4. Sopater (from Berea)
5. Aristarchus (from Thessalonica)
6. Secundus (from Thessalonica)

A Life Changing Experience in Ephesus

"It happened that while Apollos was at Corinth, Paul passed through the upper country and came to Ephesus, and found some disciples." – Acts 19:1 (NASB)

According to Acts 19, when Paul arrives in Ephesus he encountered twelve disciples that had received the baptism of John, but knew nothing about Christian baptism or the Holy Spirit. After their encounter with Paul, the twelve were baptized in the name of Jesus, and through the laying on of Paul's hands, the new disciples received the Holy Spirit and began speaking in tongues.

Note: These twelve disciples, along with Aquila, Priscilla, Epaenetus, Tychicus, and Trophimus will form the core of the Ephesian church.

During the time that Paul was teaching in the Hall of Tyrannus (Acts 19:9), a great number of people from Asia came to visit the church in Ephesus and to hear Paul preach. Among that number was a wealthy business man, named Philemon, from Colosse; who also had a slave named Onesimus. Philemon becomes a believer under Paul's teaching and stays to help Paul before heading back to Colosse. Around the same time, another man from Colosse comes to Ephesus, named Epaphras. Epaphras is converted and stays in Ephesus to be trained by Paul before going back to Colosse.

Note: After two years of training, Paul sends the eight men that he trained throughout Asia Minor to plant churches (Acts 19:10). They are part of the seven churches of Asia.

More Than Enough Power

According to Acts 19, while Paul is in Ephesus, he publicly displays extraordinary powers through the miracles that he performed. The people of Ephesus were so impressed with his power that they took his handkerchiefs from him and laid them on the sick and demon possessed and cured them. These miracles caused many magicians to be converted and burn their magical book.

Ironically, some Jews, specifically, the sons of Sceva, who observed the power that Paul displayed in the miracles when using the name of Jesus tried to imitate Paul and attempted to cast out demons by using the power that's in the name of Jesus. However, even demons can identify a "**false believer**." For the evil spirit responded to the sons by saying, *"I recognize Jesus, and I know about Paul, but who are you?"* – Acts 19:15 (NASB). As a result, the demon-possessed man beat the seven sons of Sceva for pretending to have power that they did not have and a relationship they knew nothing about.

Note: Pride seeks Power. Humility seeks Purpose. When you seek Purpose you will be given Power. When you seek Power you invite Destruction.

A Pen and Paper

Epaphras, co-laborer of Paul's, who planted the churches in Colosse and Laodicea, sails to Rome to visit Paul to inform him of the troubles the church in Colosse and Laodicea are having. During this time, Onesimus, the slave of Philemon, runs away and runs into Epaphras. Epaphras takes Onesimus with him to meet Paul, with the hope that Paul can help Onesimus.

Epaphras gives Paul an update on the troubles that are currently plaguing the churches in Colosse, Laodicea, and Philippi. Paul now writes three letters and sends them back with Tychicus (Colossians 4:7; Ephesians 6:21). Paul writes Colossians, Philemon, and Ephesians.

Note: According to Colossians 4:9, Onesimus returns to Colosse with Tychicus and a letter to Philemon. According to church history, Onesimus became an elder in the church at Ephesus.

1

I'm Familiar,
But I Didn't Know That...

Before we walk through the book of Ephesians it is important that we become familiar with the layout and construct of the book. The book of Ephesians has six chapters that seem to be divided into two main parts: Who We Are In Christ and How To Live In Christ. The first three chapters is some of the most beautiful theological writings that you will read in the New Testament. There is a since of "awe" in the boldness in which Paul declares regarding the "power" that he himself and Christians have in the body of Christ.

In the first three chapters Paul emphatically wants the Christian to know how rich he/she is in the body of Christ. His declarative statement to the believer is, "You are somebody in Christ." When you survey the current society, you will observe that a great number of books have been written on the topic of Self-Esteem, however, when you read and understand the first three chapters of the book of Ephesians, you will experience a Self-Esteem epiphany, with great clarity of who you are in Christ.

There is more said about this one congregation than any other congregation throughout the entire New Testament. When you read Acts 19 you will discover the planting and establishment of this particular congregation. In Acts 20, there is a brief narrative where Paul left Ephesus but then returned to a town called Miletus to meet with the Ephesian elders to encourage them to be strong and guard themselves against false teachers who desire to destroy the body of Christ. He then adds another layer of indictment by telling them "wolves will come in among them," and some of the people currently with them will promote a departure from the doctrine (Acts 20:28-30).

The Apostle Paul sent one of his mentees, Timothy from Lystra, to Ephesus as the evangelist for this congregation. Paul so loved this congregation and its preacher that he later penned a letter to the evangelist; we call them 1st and 2nd Timothy. In his first letter to Timothy, shortly after his greeting to Timothy, Paul encourages him by saying, "As I urged you upon my departure for Macedonia, remain on at Ephesus so that you may instruct certain men not to teach strange doctrines, nor to pay attention to myths and endless genealogies, which give rise to mere speculation rather than furthering the administration of God which is by faith" (1 Timothy 1:3-4), a reference to his prophesy about the problems that will arise in Ephesus.

As a child of God, there is a joy we should have when reading the book of Ephesians, for it is here that we see how intrinsically woven our relationship is with God and are able to identify who "we" are in Christ, and knowing this will directly **impact** our behavior. The book of Ephesians informs you how strong you are in Christ. Knowing this, it should eradicate the false thoughts that the enemy attempts to plant in your heart, that you are "weak", when in reality, you are strong in Christ.

➤ **Note:** The enemy does not fight you over where you are. He fights you over where you are going.

Say It A Different Way

There are several metaphors that are used throughout the bible to describe the relationship between church (body) and God. Consider the following examples:

1. The church is viewed as a kingdom with Christ as the King

   "In the days of those kings the God of heaven will set up a kingdom which will never be destroyed, and that kingdom will not be left for another people; it will crush and put an end to all these kingdoms, but it will itself endure forever" (Daniel 2:44).

2. The church is viewed as a flock with Jesus as The Shepherd

   "I have other sheep, which are not of this fold; I must bring them also, and they will hear My voice; and they will become one flock with one shepherd" (John 10:16).

3. The church is viewed as a collection of branches with Christ as the True Vine

   "I am the vine, you are the branches; he who abides in Me and I in him, he bears much fruit, for apart from Me you can do nothing" (John 15:5).

There are additional metaphors used throughout the bible to describe the relationship between the church and God. Perhaps the most descriptive metaphor of the relationship between the church and God is the metaphor of the church being the "**body of Christ**," describing One Body with One Head, Jesus Christ our Lord.

The Seal of Redemption (verses 1-14)

The Apostle Paul, a Jewish rabbi convert to Christianity has been overjoyed with the spiritual blessings that have been granted to him and all those who believe that he writes to them so they will know who they are in Christ and the blessings they have. Paul, metaphorically, takes a blank canvas and paints a beautiful picture in describing the Lord's church. In fact, he states very plainly in verse three that "all spiritual blessings are in Christ" and if you want access to these blessings you must be in relationship with the blessing Giver.

This is a letter that Paul wanted every believer to read because this letter emphatically tells you who you are in Christ. And, one of the trues the letter speaks about is our "**redemption**" through the blood of Jesus. And, because we have been redeemed we also become the possessors of all spiritual blessings in the heavenly places (Ephesians 1:3). Paul writes about the spiritual blessings being intrinsically connected to our redemption through the blood of Christ, that Paul used the phrase "In Him", "In Whom", or "In the Beloved," twenty-seven times describing where all spiritual blessings exists. And, since the blessings have already been granted to us, it would be oxymoronic to ask for what you already have, but rather learn to utilize them through our faith.

Note: The blessings are spiritual, not physical. Heavenly not Earthly. Eternal not Temporary.

The Apostle Paul declares that the spiritual blessings are granted to the saints, who are also predestined to become part of the family of God through adoption. Now, it is noteworthy to mention that the "*saints*" Paul is referencing are not **dead** people who have achieved high spiritual recognition, but are very much alive. In fact, the Apostle Paul refers to the believers in this letter approximately nine times by using the word "**saint**." We should not be ashamed of the word "*saint*" or even to use it as a reference to ourselves or other believers, considering that the word saint (*hagios*) means to be set apart, consecrated, and/or sanctified; which is true for the child of God.

When Paul in verse five, said, *"He predestined us to adoption as sons…,"* he is not declaring that some people, according to *"predestination"* will be saved and rejoice in heaven, while others are predestined to endure punishment through eternal damnation, regardless of their faith and works. However, is referencing the big "God-concept" of foreknowledge, that God knows what will happen before it happens, and He can know it without causing it. For example, in Dallas, Texas, there is a highway Interstate 30 that travels in the direction of East and West. If you were in Dallas and chose to get on highway Interstate 30 traveling East, in approximately five hours you will arrive in Little Rock, Arkansas. And, the highway did not start going to the state of Arkansas when you decided to get on it. In other words, highway Interstate 30 East, from Dallas, is **"predestined"** to lead to Little Rock, Arkansas, whether you decide to get on the highway or not. So, when Paul makes the statement, *"He predestined us to adoption as sons…"* he is *"metaphorically* saying when we decide to get on the spiritual highway Interstate 30 East, we become part of the already travelers and are destined to go where the road has been going, before we were born.

Twice the Lord's…

When the Apostle Paul writes that all born-again believers have been granted all spiritual blessings in the heavenly places, he describes the innate connection to us being **"redeemed"** through the blood of Jesus Christ. In other words, all the spiritual blessings given to us are the result of our redemption. Paul so wanted his readers to understand the blessings are spiritual, not material, heavenly, not earthly, eternal, not temporary, that when he writes to his original audience, he woven the two concepts of spiritual blessings and redemption as an inseparable state of being.

Note: When reading Ephesians 1 verse 3 through 14 in our English bibles, you are reading **one** sentence in the Greek text.

Embedded in verses three through fourteen, the Apostle Paul wants his original readers and us to appreciate that once upon a time in our walk that we all were servants to sin. And, during our servitude to sin, we continuously missed the mark set before us, we were transgressors of the Law of God, and we were **carriers** of a disease to which we had no cure. Unfortunately, when our hearts have been distracted by the enemy of God, there is a tendency for us to attempt to justify our behavior and develop our own concept of righteousness. However, you cannot be covered by your own righteousness. The covering we need for our "**unrighteousness**" comes from above and Paul states it is obtained through our redemption in Christ.

Note: When you become the standard of your own righteousness, you are experiencing "Self Righteousness."

The Apostle Paul declares to his original audience and to us that self-righteousness will not cover sin, for it will take sinless blood to cover our mistakes. It is essential to have the right covering in order to cover our sins. Even from the beginning of time, as we know it, having the right covering was organic. For example, in Genesis 3, Moses records the story that is referred to as the fall of mankind to sin, due to their disobedience, and in verse seven he writes, "*Then the eyes of both of them were opened, and they knew that they were naked; and they sewed fig leaves together and made themselves loin coverings.*" Look at the parallel of the importance of having the right covering in

Ephesians 1, with blood, and the need for a covering in Genesis 3, which will also require blood.

In Genesis 3, Adam and Eve recognized they were naked and attempted to "cover" themselves in their own righteousness and made fig leaves as a covering. Unfortunately, the covering of fig leaves cannot redeem you from sin. They needed the cover that only comes from God so it could redeem them from their sins. In Genesis 3 and verse 21, Moses records, "*The Lord God made garments of skin for Adam and his wife, and clothed them.*" Observe that God sacrificed the life of animal to obtain an appropriate covering for Adam and Eve; the right covering to redeem them back to God. So, when nobody can pay the price for redemptions, God paid the price. And from that point, God instituted the killing of animals to be used as a sacrifice.

Note: In Genesis 3, God shed blood and sacrificed the life of an animal to give His children the right covering for redemption. This was a foreshadowing of a time when He will sacrifice the life of His Only Begotten Son, and through His blood make a covering that can redeem us from sin. John the Baptist referred to Him as the "**Lamb of God**" (John 1:29).

The Apostle Paul declares that we are "**redeemed**" through the blood of Jesus Christ. The word redeemed (redemption) means to be purchased out of the slave market. Jesus purchased us out of the slave market of "sin," making us twice the Lord's. The concept of being twice the Lord's is a parallel to a story about a young boy, who at the age of twelve, made a small toy sail boat with his own hands, using the skills he had obtained from watching his father. The story narrates that one day the boy took the boat out to the lake to see if it could float and sail. He was overjoyed when the boat could float, however, a strong wind came and pushed the boat too far into the water for the young boy to retrieve the boat. The story says the young boy went home in tears and with a broken heart.

Three weeks later, the young boy and his father were walking downtown on Main Street and came to a pawn shop and the young boy saw his boat through the window of the store. As they entered the store, the young boy shouted, "That's my boat. I made it with my own hands," to which the salesman responded, "Whether it's your boat or not I do not know, but if you want it you have to pay five dollars." The young boy paid the cost and went outside and held his boat up high and said with joy, "You are twice mine. You are mine because I made you and you are mine because I purchased you back."

Note: We are twice the Lord's. We are His because He made us and we are His because He purchased us back, buying us from the slave market of sin.

‑ We are redeemed through the blood of Jesus Christ and as a result our sins are covered with the right covering. This allows us to receive a pardon from our sins, not because we are innocent, but because we have been purchased out of the slave market of sin and now have access to all spiritual blessings in the heavenly places. In addition, the believer is sealed with the Holy Spirit of promise, with a guaranteed inheritance (verses 13-14). The word "seal" carries the idea that the believer is authenticated and is the possessor of the certificate of genuiness. And, to be "sealed" by the Holy Spirit is our "deposit" from God, guaranteeing our inheritance of salvation in heaven. Therefore, we do not have to ask for the blessings, for God has already given them to us. We just need to utilize the access and power that we have in Jesus Christ.

Note: The Triune God is directly participating in "sealing" every be-

feel good
but necessary being good
not tried to emotion
looking for fight
but not righteous
Phil 4:8

liever. God the Father seals, God the Son is the domain in which the **seal** takes places, and God the Holy Spirit is the Agent of the seal.

Four Times The Power (15 – 23)

Beginning in verse fifteen, the Apostle Paul shifts his focus from encouraging the believer to embrace his/her access to all spiritual blessings through the redemption they have obtained, to exalting the supreme power given to the believer through Jesus. Now, there is a difference between being the possessor of power and knowing how to use the power that you possess. Learning to exercise the power granted to you through the Holy Spirit is predicated upon whether you understand the true "**hope**" of His calling of you. The concept of "hope" in Scripture is a reference to the absolute certainty of a believer's victory in God. And, as a result when life presents interruptions, distractions, dysfunctions, and delays in your journey, you can with absolute certainty invoke the power that you have in Jesus to sustain you through the inconvenient moments of life.

To express how powerful the believer is, in verse nineteen, the Apostle Paul, four times, using four different words, describes the power given to us through seal of the Holy Spirit. Notice verse nineteen, "*and what is the surpassing greatness of His power toward us who believe. These are in accordance with the working of the strength of His might…*" Now, it may not be obvious to you as you read it, but taking our time to understand the verse, you will recognize that we have "**Four Times The Power**" in Christ. The first time the word is used in verse nineteen is the word "**power**." This word "power" is the Greek word "*dynamis*," which is where we obtain our English word "dynamite," and it describes an innate supernatural, miracle working kind of power that belongs to God alone and He directs this power toward the believer. The second time the word is used in this verse is the word "**working**." This word "working" is the Greek word "*energe-*

ian," which is where we derive our English word "energy." The third time the word is used in this verse is the word "**strength**," derived from the Greek word "*kratos*," a reference to God's sovereignty. And, the fourth time this word is used in this verse is the word "**might**," a translation from the Greek word "*ischys*," describing an unlimited and unrestricted amount of spiritual and physical power that God has and His ability to overcome any resistance. In other words, the Apostle Paul states in this verse that the God we serve has Power, Power, Power, Power.

This tremendous expression of the **Power** that is made available to all believers highlight that a Christian does not just have power, but has "**Four Times**" the power and Paul demonstrates three expressions of this power that are seen in Christ. The first is the "**working**" (energeian) power that conquered the grave and raised Jesus from the dead. It was God's energetic that accomplished this resurrection and this same "**working**" power is made available to the Christian today. The second expression of power is all things are subject under His feet (Ephesians 1:22). And, the third manifestation of power is Christ is "***head over all things to the church, which is His body, the fullness of Him who fills all in all***" (Ephesians 1:22-23).

Note: When you know your worth in Jesus Christ and the power granted you, will not walk with your head hung low, but walk upright, allowing your thinking to influence your emotions, yielding healthier behavior.

Know my worth
understand the hope

Spiritual Anatomy (20-23)

The Apostle Paul, after describing the four types of power that exists in Christ, which are also available to the believer, through the seal of the Holy Spirit, Paul now gives the divine definition and anatomy of the church (*ekklesia*) by making it synonymous with the Body of

((When you know your worth" in Jesus Christ (Eph1:19) Same resurrection power in me / You know the power granted you

Christ. And, he uses the illustration of a physical body to provide insight to the spiritual body, the church. He analogizes how the physical body has one head, the same is true for the spiritual body, and Christ is made the One Head over one Body, His church, and this Body is His fullness.

Consider what it means for the body to be the fullness of Christ through the illustration the Apostle Paul uses to the church in Colosse, which meets in Philemon's house. In Colossians 2:8-10, it reads, "*See to it that no one takes you captive through philosophy and empty deception, according to the tradition of men, according to the elementary principles of the world, rather than according to Christ. For in Him all the fullness of Deity dwells in bodily form, and in Him you have been made complete, and He is the head over all rule and authority…*" For example, my son, who is now married and has his own son, is the physical expression of who I am. He is my fullness. He looks like me, talks like me, walks like me, and in many cases, he even thinks like me. He is the physical expression of everything that I am. In the same way, Christ is the fullness of the Godhead, expressed in bodily form. Jesus is a theophany of the Father, Word, and Spirit. And, since the church is His body, then the church must be everything Christ represents. In order for the church to be the fullness of Christ it is non-negotiable that the church looks like Him, talks like Him, walks like Him, and even thinks like Him.

Note: A theophany is a physical expression of Deity.

2

Life After Death (1-7)

*"And you were dead in your trespasses and sins, in which you formerly walked according to the course of this world, according to the prince of the power of the air, of the spirit that is now working in the sons of disobedience. Among them we too all formerly lived in the lusts of our flesh, indulging the desires of the flesh and of the mind, and were by **nature** children of wrath, even as the rest. **But God**, being rich in mercy, because of His great love with which He loved us, even when we were dead in our transgressions, made us alive together with Christ (by grace you have been saved), and raised us up with Him, and seated us with Him in the heavenly places in Christ Jesus, so that in the ages to come He might show the surpassing riches of His grace in kindness toward us in Christ Jesus"* (Ephesians 2:1-7) – NASB.

Before we continue with the applicational transition in the Apostle Paul's thought process, as he starts, what our canonical bible refers to as *"Chapter 2,"* let's do a quick overview of Chapter One. In the last five verses of Chapter One, beginning with verse 19, four times the Apostle describes how powerful we are, as believers, in Christ, and solidifies that we have access to the same Power that raised Jesus from the dead. He then closes the chapter with verses 22 and 23, showing the Power Christ has over all things, related to the church, and through the metaphor proclaims it to be His body, with Jesus as the Head.

The declarative of Jesus having all Power over all things and the imagery of the church being His body, should be to us what the crossing of the Red Sea was to Israel. Whenever God wanted to refer to His demonstration of Power He would say, *"AM I not the God that brought you across the Red Sea and delivered you from Pharaoh and all your enemies, while you watched them drown in the sea"* (Exodus 14:13; Joshua 24:6). And from generation to generation when Israel thought about the Power of God, they referenced back to the Passover and the crossing of the Red Sea; which both demonstrates God's Power and love for His people. This became their foundational point of reference from which their faith stood.

Note: What the Passover and Red Sea crossing was to the Old Testament church, Jesus being raised from the dead is to the New Testament church.

The Apostle Paul emphatically states that you cannot know Jesus' exceeding greatness and power without referring back to Jesus being raised from the dead, for death was the greatest enemy that we would have to confront. However, when Jesus was raised from the dead, He proved forever that He is not Lord over some things, but He is Lord over all things (Ephesians 1:22), which becomes the reference point for our faith, **resurrection from the dead**.

So, when Paul brings closure to his thought about the Power that is in Christ, in Chapter 2, he makes application of his thought by introducing the concept of "being raised from the dead," while death is still fresh on the mind of his readers. He pens in verse one of chapter 2, "*And you were dead in your trespasses and sins…*" It almost seems oxymoronic that Paul would say to these Christians, who are followers of Jesus, that they were **dead**. Yes, it would be somewhat shocking for someone to walk up to you and say, "by the way you were dead." For, the surprised response may be, "*I was?*"

The Apostle Paul informs his readers then and now, you were dead in your trespasses and sins, until He made you alive. The principle Paul wants his readers to see is they were dead in the most significant way; they were dead **inwardly**. They seemed to be alive outwardly but they were dead inwardly. What Paul is describing is a heart issue. The death he is referring to is not physical death, but spiritual death. In other words, the natural man is alive in his fleshly body but he is dead in his spirit. For example, recall in Genesis 2, verses 16 and 17, God told Adam, "*From any tree of the garden you may eat freely; but from the tree of the knowledge of good and evil you shall not eat, for in the day that you eat from it you will surely die.*" And, as the narrative goes, eventually, both Eve and Adam ate fruit from the forbidden tree, and immediately they died. They experienced a spiritual death.

Note: Physical death is the separation of the soul from the body. Spiritual death is the separation of the soul from God.

When you come to know God, it is through your spirit, for God is Spirit. Our relationship with God is not based on having a fleshly experience, knowing that God is not a "natural" lover, but a lover of the inner most part of our being. However, when sin is present our spirit is silenced by sin, thus we are dead in our trespasses and sins. In the bible, the word "death" never means the cessation of life but simply a separation. Physical death is the separation of the spirit from the body. For the Christian, to be absent in the body is to be present with the Lord (2 Corinthians 5:8). The spirit continues to live somewhere, though it is separated from the body. Spiritual death is the separation of the spirit from God. Without God's Spirit our spirit is dead. However, when God takes up residence in our bodies and breathes into our spirit we become "**alive**" in our inner most parts.

Note: Trespasses means to take false steps. Sins means to fall by the wayside. Slightly different in their root meaning but when used together it suggests deliberate acts that we do against God and His righteousness.

In the opening of Chapter 2, the Apostle Paul is looking back at his past and the past of his original readers and indirectly asked the question, "Do you realize that you were dead?" Living your life, but walking around dead? Buying property dead? Going to school dead? Getting married dead? Because there are two things against you, "*trespasses*" and "*sins*." In other words, you have done a myriad of things but you really were not living at all. Perhaps that is why some people need a great number of stimuli and influences in order to feel alive. When this is the case, some will try to find it in a bottle, drugs, sex, et cetera. This is the trap of the enemy and when you are dead in your spirit, he attempts to convince you that the only way for you to get any impulses and satisfy the cravings in your life is to do the things that make you feel alive; even though it is destructive.

There is a "hollow" feeling in being dead in your spirit. However, when Christ comes and takes up residence within you, He resuscitates you from the death of your sin. And now you can look back over your past life, reminisce over what you did when you were dead, but celebrate that now you are made alive in Christ. Paul then reminds his readers in verse two of the walk they had, "*according to the course of this world, according to the prince of the power of the air…*" The phrase, "according to" means "in harmony to." The Apostle Paul wants his readers to come face-to-face with their reality and not pretend like they do not know what it is like to walk according to this world. He suggests in his phrase, not only did you walk the walk but you enjoyed when you walked. And the beat of the drum you walked to was "**in harmony**" with the prince of the power of the air, who is Satan. And during your dead-man walking marathon, it was the spirit of the evil one that directed your steps. It was the spirit that is now working in the sons of disobedience that use to encourage you to live out your own lusts, according to your own will, after all, by "**nature**" you were the children of wrath, just like the rest of us.

The Apostle Paul, metaphorically, takes a blank canvas and paints a beautiful picture that demonstrates a then-now lifestyle, recognizing that it takes time to eradicate the "then" in-order for the "now" to become your norm. Consider Israel coming out of Egypt. After 430 years of being enslaved, they come out, but it took forty years to get the influence of Egypt out of them. Thus, Paul encourages his readers in their then-now state of being, that now you have been made alive, you want to grow to a state-of-being where you no longer respond to the world systems the same way you did when you were dead in your trespasses and sins. Being made alive encourages you not to respond to anger, frustrations, disappointment, and many more emotional presence, like someone who is dead in their spirit.

Note: When you are made alive in Christ you are no longer controlled by the generational curses of this world.

The way you break the cycle of dysfunction and generational curses is to be made alive in your spirit. However, if you resist to be renewed in your spirit, no amount of encouragement, preaching, or spiritual activities is going to correct a **heart issue**. One of the reasons that is a true statement is because no one can legislate morality. You cannot pass a bill via the government that will make people love one another. That is a **heart issue**. However, people who are interested in being made alive in their spirit will have to consciously make the choice to lose the chains of this world and start **inwardly** with their heart.

In verse three, *"Among them we too all formerly lived in the lusts of our flesh, indulging the desires of the flesh and of the mind, and were by nature children of wrath, even as the rest,"* Paul connects with his readers by saying, we were all there, locked up in the cravings of our own body. It is important to note that we all came into this physical world with the "**potential**" to sin. Nobody had to teach the toddler to tell untruths. For example, consider the young toddler has been caught with his hand in the cookie jar and cookie crumbs around his mouth. When his/her mother or father ask if they have been in the cookie jar, especially if they were instructed not to eat any, the quick response from the child is "no ma'am" or "no sir." Why would the toddler give this response? The child did not attend any "lying seminars" or listen to "How to lie" audiobooks, but inevitably under pressure, lying comes out of the toddler. Why? Because it is down inside of them.

So, in verse three, the Apostle Paul describes the depth of our former lives. We are in the basement of our lust and desires and metaphorically, Paul comes and kicks the door open and says, "It was not just you, but all of us have had our conversations in times past." He is making it clear to his readers that he is not talking down to them, but letting them know he can identify with them, for he has "been" them.

In verse four, the Apostle Paul changes his direction when he says, *"But God..."* This is the turning point to flesh depravity; But God. There are no other solutions for racial prejudices and injustices; But God. No other satisfaction for the craving of the flesh; But God. There is no other healing for the broken heart and loneliness, or healing for the angry spirit that you love; But God. God is the turning point in our story. Paul declares, *"But God, being rich in mercy, because of His great love with which He loved us..."*

Note: God is rich in mercy and then spent it on us.

In verse five, the Apostle Paul gives us a celebratory statement when he said, *"even when we were dead in our transgressions, made us alive together with Christ (by grace you have been saved)."* That statement alone is worth a shout. What Paul is describing in this verse is the process of God bringing the church together, both Jews and Gentiles. He declares it will not be two separate nations living under one government, but will be reconciled into one nation, one body. Paul's whole mission is to demonstrate that although we may have different backgrounds, we are raised up **together**. Paul understood how it is possible that the Jews could see themselves as the ones to lead this movement, after all, they have years of religious background found throughout the Old Testament. But Paul makes it clear that God did not raise you up separately but raised you up together. Raise up from what? That low place we just got through talking about. That is a true resurrection in the life of the believer.

In verse six he says, *"and raised us up with Him, and seated us with Him in the heavenly places in Christ Jesus…"* In a very simple way, the Apostle Paul acknowledges two powerful **motions**. In one motion, He raised us up. And, in another motion He seated us with Him. In verse seven he tells us why He did it when he writes, *"so that in the ages to come He might show the surpassing riches of His grace in kindness toward us in Christ Jesus."* In other words, God wants to bless you and He will even use your past to help bless you. The God of all creation knew when He saved you that there were some people who knew something about your past. And, He is going to use what was against you to now work for you for His glory. For example, consider the lame man in John 5 when Jesus told him, *"Get up, pickup your pallet and walk."* The picture Jesus is painting is the thing that was carrying you, the pallet, you are now able to carry it. Look at how much God can do with so little.

Note: It is hard to fathom how God made us out of clay. Something that would even hold water.

The Family Union (8-13)

"For by grace you have been saved through faith; and that not of yourselves, it is the gift of God; not as a result of works, so that no one may boast. For we are His workmanship, created in Christ Jesus for good works, which God prepared beforehand so that we would walk in them. Therefore remember that formerly you, the Gentiles in the flesh, who are called 'Uncircumcision' by the so-called 'Circumcision,' which is performed in the flesh by human hands—remember that you were at that time separate from Christ, excluded from the commonwealth of Israel, and strangers to the covenants of promise, having no hope and without God in the world. But now in Christ Jesus you who formerly were far off have been brought near by the blood of Christ" (Ephesians 2:8-13).

Through this collection of verses, the Apostle Paul makes it clear that we understand the salvation granted to us is not based upon us obeying enough rules or our own righteousness, but it is the **gift** of God. An important note to understand about gifts, is a gift does not cost the receiver anything. But, it does cost the giver. As it relates to our salvation, it is the gift of God and it cost God the very life of His Son.

Note: For by grace you have been saved through faith. Grace is God's part. Faith is our part.

Between verses eight through twelve, the Apostle Paul used a number of adjectives to describe the spiritual condition of a Gentile believer. He referred to them as strangers, aliens, and from a distance perspective, far off or way out there. However, it is in verse twelve that truly defines verse one and what it means to be dead in your trespasses and sins. In verse twelve he pens, "*remember that you were at that time separate from Christ, excluded from the commonwealth of Israel, and strangers to the covenants of promise, having no hope and without God in the world.*" To be in the world and not have a relationship with your Creator is a terrible and hopeless position. But God... The same people, who were once ridiculed, overlooked, considered second class citizens and heathens, by the Jewish born believer are now invited into the same house and eating at the same table of the Jewish believer. In verse thirteen Paul writes, "*But now in Christ Jesus you who formerly were far off have been brought near by the blood of Christ.*" The Gentile believer, through the blood of Christ has now been brought into a relationship of intimacy with God. Paul is celebrating the "**position**" of the believer in Christ. He is trying to teach us to not focus on the temporal but to prefer the eternal.

The first readers of Paul's letter did not view death in the same way that it is so often viewed today. Even the Apostle Paul, when he wrote to the church in Philippi, he declared, "*But I am hard-pressed from both directions, having the desire to depart and be with Christ, for that is very much better; yet to remain on in the flesh is more necessary for your sake*" (Philippians 1:23-24). This would be comically equivalent to a saint today saying, "I don't know if I should go be with the Lord or stay here and teach bible class." Their perspective of death was viewed with a more in-depth lens that projected "eternity" as real living and this world as temporary. Unfortunately, it seems today the concepts have been reversed. Believers have fallen in love with this world, something that is only temporary. But, because we have been existing in this world for so long, the enemy has deceived some in believing that they are "earthly," not appreciating that we are spiritual beings who simply having a physical experience. However, this too shall pass.

Note: When you fall in love with the world, you get excited about

God's ability to alter your **conditions**, without every mentioning your **position**.

Broken Barriers (14-18)

> "For He Himself is our peace, who made both groups into one and broke down the barrier of the dividing wall, by abolishing in His flesh the enmity, which is the Law of commandments contained in ordinances, so that in Himself He might make the two into one new man, thus establishing peace, and might reconcile them both in one body to God through the cross, by it having put to the death the enmity. And He came and preached peace to you who were far away, and peace to those who were near; for through Him we both have our access in one Spirit to the Father."

The Apostle Paul declares that Jesus broke down the thing that stood between the Jews and Gentiles being part of the same family, and that was the Law. So, if the Law was the dividing wall between Jews and Gentiles, then what was the purpose of the Law? It is important to understand that the Law was "ordained" by the angels (Galatians 3:19), who were representatives of God and given to Moses, who was the representative of the people. Two mediators of a Law that was never designed to bring eternal life, but serve as sin barometer until the Seed (Galatians 3:16) came, after which it was no longer needed. Jesus replaced the use of two mediators and became the Mediator of a new covenant that was established on better promises (Hebrews 8:6) and broke down the barrier of race and religion by dying on a cross.

Note: It is ironic how Jesus tore down walls to bring racially divided people together, while some are motivated to build up walls to keep racially divided people apart.

When the Apostle Paul writes, and informs the Gentile believers that Jesus died, in order to remove the barrier of the Law, that they may become part of the one family of God, he was telling them that God had established true faith on a higher principle. However, you can imagine when a Jewish believer, whom believed they had exclusive access to God, in the region of Ephesus read Paul's words about the Law no longer being required, would resist the words of Paul; not just because the Law was important to them, but they could not imagine being in the same family with the 'uncircumcised' Gentiles.

One of the claims of fame to the Jews in first century Palestine, and many today, is the idea of being the descendants of Abraham. In John 8, Jesus is in a dialogue with some Law keeping Jews who claim to be children of Abraham, in which Jesus would claim, Abraham was made righteous, but not by the Law. In fact, Abraham lived before the Law and before circumcision, and was found justified before God. Not only that, Abraham was **not even** Hebrew. He was a Gentile, who by faith, believed God and it was credited to him as righteousness (Romans 4:3). Therefore, if God could justify Gentile Abraham, surely, He can break down the barrier and justify you and me in the same family.

In verse eighteen he states, *"for through Him we both have our access in one Spirit to the Father."* In other words, Jesus provides both, Jew and Gentile, access to the Father through the same Spirit. And, when you know you have access to the Father you can talk to Him with confidence because you have access.

Note: Praying to God while doubting if He hears you, is like a child ringing the doorbell to get access to the house where they live. You don't have to ring the door bell, because you have access. Why are you ringing the bell when Jesus died to give you the key?

Construction In Process (19-22)

"So then you are no longer strangers and aliens, but you are fellow citizens with the saints, and are of God's household, having been built on the foundation of the apostles and prophets, Christ Jesus Himself being the corner stone, in whom the whole building, being fitted together, is growing into a holy temple in the Lord, in whom you also are being built together into a dwelling of God in the Spirit."

The Apostle Paul, again, encourages the Gentile believers and us alike, that we have become fellow citizens with the saints. This reference to fellow citizens with the saints includes the redeemed of all ages beginning with Adam, and even reaching back into eternity past with the angelic host who are in heaven. For Paul will later say to this same group of believers, *"For this reason I bow my knees before the Father, from whom every* **family** *in heaven and on earth derives its name…"* (Ephesians 3:14-15).

In the process of removing barrier wall and metaphorically reconstructing a new building, Paul states, there is a secret to being fitted together (Ephesians 2:21). One observation, if you are not growing in your spiritual journey, it is an indicator that you are not fitted together. For you cannot be independent and a member of the body. On the other hand, if you are fitted together properly, you will grow. Jesus fits us together. It is like finding different rocks but getting the right shapes and then fit them together. However, here within we find the struggle, and the enemy knows that you struggle with it. Now, you can offer praise to God by yourself. But, there is a level of worship that you can only have when you come together with the body of Christ.

Collective worship releases a level of praise and glory that will outshine anything you can do alone. That is why the enemy fights with you, trying to keep you in conflict with other believers. Now, the enemy will not fight you or try to distract you in having a relationship with God, but he does not want you to have a healthy relationship with other believers, because if you cannot connect across a room of believers, then the enemy knows you cannot build a wall. But, if you make connections and you are **fitted** together, you become a defense system against the enemy and a habitation for God in the spirit.

The phrase "a habitation for God in the spirit" is the canvas to paint a picture of the temple. Consider this... When the people of Israel would travel with the Ark of the Covenant, they would move it and the tabernacle by caring it on the shoulders of men, using staves. When they stopped, they would setup the tabernacle and the presence of God would come to them. And God's commitment to His people was, 'as long as you're moving by yourself, I AM with you.' However, when they carried the Ark of the Covenant to the Temple of Solomon, they removed the staves, indicating they will not be moving anymore. Metaphorically, God is saying, if you want my anointing to rest upon you, then pull the staves out and I will stay with you.

We are fitted together. When believers get together there is a level of spiritual worship that occurs that the enemy cannot stop, so he attempts to stop believers from getting together. So, if he prevents you from getting together collectively with the believers, you will still experience individual blessings, but the greater release of worship and anointing is when we are **fitted together**, to lessen the impact and influence of the enemy. As a note of reference, there was one time when Jesus complimented Satan, and that was for his unity. While debating with the Pharisees on the claim that His miracles of casting out demons was by the power of Satan, in which Jesus replied, *"Any kingdom divided against itself is laid waste; and a house divided against itself falls"* (Luke 11:17). He indicated that Satan is unified. Legion is a group of demons who are unified, working together.

Note: You will never read in all the history of scripture of two demons fighting each other, because his kingdom is united. However, you will read about all kinds of believers fighting against one another.

Satan's last hope in overthrowing the purity of our faith is predicated upon our disunity. The enemy knows that whenever believers get together there is a release of a level of God's glory, and God declares, 'I'll dwell in the midst, not of a person, but of My people,' because He has raised us up together.

we have freedom but don't believe -
legions dont have freedom but believe
they are free - no rules

3

It's Not a Secret.
It's a Mystery (1-13)

"For this reason I, Paul, the prisoner of Christ Jesus for the sake of you Gentiles—if indeed you have heard of the stewardship of God's grace which was given to me for you; that by revelation there was made known to me the mystery, as I wrote before in brief. By referring to this, when you read you can understand my insight into the mystery of Christ, which in other generations was not made known to the sons of men, as it has now been revealed to His holy apostles and prophets in the Spirit; to be specific, that the Gentiles are fellow heirs and fellow members of the body, and fellow partakers of the promise in Christ Jesus through the gospel, of which I was made a minister, according to the gift of God's grace which was given to me according to the working of His power. To me, the least of all saints, this grace was given, to preach to the Gentiles the unfathomable riches of Christ, and to bring to light what is the administration of the mystery which for ages has been hidden in God

who created all things; so that the manifold wisdom of God might now be made known through the church to the rulers and the authorities in the heavenly places. This was in accordance with the eternal purpose which He carried out in Christ Jesus our Lord, in whom we have boldness and confident access through faith in Him. Therefore I ask you not to lose heart at my tribulations on your behalf, for they are your glory (Ephesians 3:1-13) – NASB.

Prior to the words penned by the Apostle Paul, in what is referred to as "Chapter 3," he has been preoccupied with describing the works of Jesus and what He has done to sanctify the church. In the previous chapters he has defined the church and he has defined the role of the believer. He has taught the believer about their wealth and worship in Christ. Now, as we journey through Chapter 3, the Apostle Paul begins talking about his role in the church. He begins by identifying himself and his purpose in the church and shares with his original listeners what he wants them to know.

The way he describes himself and his role in the church in this Chapter gives a strong indication that he has matured beyond his impressive biological and educational background. He mentions nothing about being a descendent of the tribe of Benjamin; the tribe of the kings. He says nothing about being a Hebrew of Hebrews, a Pharisee, or being a persecutor of the church. If the Apostle Paul wanted to impress his readers he could easily do that. He was above his peers in his intelligence. Prolific in his writings. He was well diverse in multicultural experiences and spoke multiple languages. The Apostle Paul was known by all of the scholars and theologians of his day, and highly respected by them, **until** he became a Christian.

Once he became a Christian, the Apostle found himself in an

educational dilemma, because he was an **intelligent** Christian; which is considered an oxymoron to the thinkers of his day. To the Jewish scholar, Christians were thought to be insane, because they believed in a "Savior" that died and risen from the dead. And if that is not enough, the audacity of the Christians to suggest the Messiah had come and Israel had missed Him was absolutely ridiculous to the Jewish scholar. It would be expected for someone like, the Apostle Peter to teach the concept of a "resurrected Savior," because he was an unlearned man, according to their standards. But, for Paul, a Pharisee amongst Pharisees, trained by the Gamaliel, to teach Jesus as the Messiah was quick to be rejected by his contemporaries.

So, in the first two chapters of the book of Ephesians, the Apostle Paul has engulfed himself with the personage of Jesus Christ and who we are in Him, that the Apostle over looks his family heritage, his educational pedigree, and simply says… *"For this reason I, Paul, the prisoner of Christ Jesus for the sake of you Gentiles"* (Ephesians 3:1). While he was in his hometown in Cilicia, he had a profound spiritual experience that was so incredulous, that he was not sure if he was taken out of his body or not. What he does know is somehow he ascended to the third Heaven and saw and heard things that are unlawful for a man to repeat (2 Corinthians 12:1-14). He called it **mysteries** and did not speak about until fourteen years later; making him a prisoner of Christ Jesus.

In verses one and two, he declares that his God-given assignment is to proclaim the gospel to the Gentiles. What a humbling job for a man who was **extremely** Jewish. He was so proud of his Hebrew lineage that he was killing people that rose up against Judaism. Ironically, Jesus does not commission him to the Jewish scholars, to debate the Law, but He sends him to the idolatrous Gentile nations. Being sent to the Gentiles required the Apostle Paul to travel to places like Rome. During Paul's day, Rome would have been the equivalent to the *Red-light* district in Los Angeles California. It was one of the most loose moral cities in that day; plagued with polygamy and incestualize relationships. It is to this type of culture that God made Paul an Apostle.

Note: The Apostle Paul is now sitting and teaching people that he would not have talked to prior to his conversion.

For three years the Apostle Paul has been the voice and teacher for the believers in Ephesus, sitting and revealing the mystery of Jesus Christ. He has been given the task of handling the **mystery**, and the **mystery** he unfolds is God's timeless plan that He hid in His Son, to have fellowship with a people not yet created. Put another way, God desires to produce a community on earth that will reflect the community that exists among the Father, Word (Son), and the Spirit. This community is now known as the "**ekklesia**," the Greek word translated "church" in our English bibles.

Now, this **mystery**, from a Jewish perspective was unfathomable. In verse three, he pens, "*that by revelation there was made known to me the mystery, as I wrote before in brief.*" He makes reference to what we now know as the church, but the Jews thought the concept of a church to be far-fetched and a made up theology by the Christians. Now, before we judge the Jewish thinker too quickly for rejecting this "church" idea, consider how you would feel if someone in your family, that you watched grow up, matriculate through elementary school, junior high, and even high school, and then come to the family reunion and shout out loud that they were God in the flesh. And then require you to bow down and worship them? It was confusing to the Jewish thinker. Yes, they were waiting for "something" from God, but not "somebody" born in a manger.

When looking at the God-given ministry for the Apostle Paul, we get to see the epitome of humility. The Jesus that he use to laugh at, it is this **same** Jesus he now serves as a prisoner and preaches this ridiculous Jesus to those ridiculous Gentiles. And, to further complicate his ministry, the Apostle Paul is preaching a concept that he calls the **mystery**, something he had little Old Testament validation, but through his ministry he continues to teach **mysteries**. For example, in 1 Corinthians 15:51 he writes, *"Behold, I tell you a mystery; we will not all sleep, but we will all be changed..."* And, again in 1 Timothy 3:16, he writes to Timothy, his son in the gospel, *"...great is the mystery of godliness: He who was revealed in the flesh, Was vindicated in the Spirit, Seen by angels, Proclaimed among the nations, Believed on in the world, Taken up in glory."*

Note: The Apostle Paul's entire ministry was threaded with **mysteries**. And, although the Old Testament saints and believers in Jesus believed in the resurrection from the dead, Paul now is telling them through the **mystery**, 'you don't have to die to be changed' and 'we shall not all sleep but shall be changed.' The Jewish community rejected his teaching, so God sent him to the Gentiles.

We observe in verses four through six that God has invited the Gentiles to eat at the same table as the Jews, and to the Jew, that was mind boggling because they could not comprehend how that could be the case. The Apostle Paul says, the reason you don't understand it is because it is a **mystery**. And, since the Gentiles have been invited, by God, to sit at the same table as the Jews, metaphorically, now comes the lame, sick, and lepers to a white linen dinner table, to sit and eat at a table prepared for Aristocrats. No wonder the Jews don't know what to think about this **mystery**. God has broken all protocol in the method He chose to save us. In other words, God broke all etiquette when He called for all "heathens" to be filled with His Spirit, and the Apostle calls it "The Mystery."

When comparing his past life experiences and behaviors before encountering Christ on the Damascus road (Acts 9:1-6), how he stood in agreement with those who stoned Stephen, and he himself traveled from house after house, dragging men and women to prison (Acts 7:54-8:3). But now, as an Apostle of Jesus Christ, understanding he is not worthy of the **mercy** afforded him by God, he humbly proclaims himself to be the "very least of all saints" (Ephesians 3:7). And, to further capture his heart of thanksgiving for God's mercy, the Apostle Paul states, in spite of his past experiences and behavior, God granted him **grace** to do two things: to "preach" to the Gentiles, a race of people not considered to be worthy by the orthodox Jewish nation, and to share with the Gentiles the "unfathomable" wealth of Christ (Ephesians 3:7-8).

Note: The word "grace" in our English Bible is translated from the Greek word "χάρις" (charis), which means to be granted favor in-spite of a deserved punishment.

The Apostle's reference to the "unfathomable" wealth of Christ is another way of saying, he has discovered the *'treasure chest'* of the riches of Christ, and there are no words to express how much he has learned, based on what he has seen and heard. What he does make clear is, it is a "**mystery**." In verse nine he states, "*and to bring to light what is the administration of the mystery which for ages has been hidden in God who created all things…*" This mystery has been hidden in God, however, it was on the blueprints that God laid out, before the foundation of the world. On the blueprints, God has a plan to redeem the Gentiles, but He will first bring in the Hebrews. The Hebrews would be a first fruit offering, of which the Gentiles would become a latter day harvest. And, in the last days, God proclaims, "I will pour out My Spirit on all mankind…" (Joel 2:28).

Every now and then you see hidden in the fibers of the Old Testament the slight suggestions that salvation has always been bigger than just the nation of Israel. In other words, when reading the Old Testament, there are a few glimpses and clues suggesting that God's plan is bigger than just one group of people. The mere fact Jesus reminds His listeners that there were lepers in Naaman's day, that were part of the house of Israel, and they all died of leprosy (Luke 4:27).

Note: Naaman, who was not an Israelite, but a Syrian, was cured of leprosy, however, all the lepers of Israel died from leprosy.

Another glimpse that the **mystery** of salvation is bigger than one nation of people, Jesus states to His listeners, *"But I say to you in truth, there were many widows in Israel in the days of Elijah, when the sky was shut up for three years and six months, when a great famine came over all the land; and yet Elijah was sent to none of them, but only to Zarephath, in the land of Sidon, to a woman who was a widow"* (Luke 4:25-26). Glimpses… When Jesus encounters the Centurion, who asks Him to heal his servant, Jesus desired to go to the home of the Centurion. However, feeling unworthy, the Centurion replied, *"say the word and my servant will be healed."* Jesus responded, *"not even in Israel have I found such great faith"* (Luke 2:1-9). Again, consider the woman from Sidon who came to Jesus pleading His help for her daughter who was cruelly demon-possessed. Jesus responded by saying, *"It is not good to take the children's bread and throw it to the dogs."* And, the woman replied, *"Yes, Lord; but even dogs feed on the crumbs which fall from their masters' table."* This response moved Jesus, causing Him to say, *"O woman, your faith is great; it shall be done for you as you wish"* (Matthew 15:22-28).

The Mystery has been hidden in the mind of God and veiled throughout the bible, including the hidden glimpses mentioned above, and now the Apostle Paul exposes and reveals that God has always had a plan that included all people, not just Israel. And, while the Jews may stand and ponder, 'How can these Gentiles be brought to the same table,' whereby the Apostle informs them, 'The same God that brought something out of nothing, spoke the Gentiles to the table, the same way He spoke the Jews to the table.' What was hidden in verses eight and nine is now revealed in verse 10, *"so that the manifold wisdom of God might now be made known through the church to the rulers and the authorities in the heavenly places."*

Note: When the Apostle Paul uses the terms rulers (principalities) and authorities (powers) in verse ten, he is not referencing earthly beings or some form of government, but rather he is referencing two ranks of angels. After all, he says, "rulers and the authorities in the heavenly places." There are at least nine ranks of angels mentioned in our canon of the scriptures. The following makeup the nine:

Seraphim	Cherubim	Thrones
Dominion	Principalities	Powers
Virtues	Archangels	Angels

Now Is The Time

The Apostle Paul proclaims that now is the time for the **mystery** to be revealed. There is a time and purpose for everything that occurs. God does not reveal everything in one moment. He reveals it in stages. The evolution of knowledge is progressive and ongoing. For example, God reveals that salvation and reconciliation will come through the Lamb, however, He does not give it to us all at once. In Genesis during the sacrifices offered by Cain and Abel, it is Abel that gave a blood sacrifice by offering a lamb, but we don't know anything about the lamb until we read the book of Exodus.

In Exodus 12 we are to identify some characteristics of the lamb. The lamb is to be without spot or blemish, a male lamb, and the blood of the lamb is to be applied to the doorpost of the believer. Additional characteristics of the lamb are mentioned in Isaiah 53, *"Behold, He is like a lamb that is led to the slaughter."* Now we understand that not only is it to be a lamb without spot or blemish, but the lamb is to be a man. However, we don't know what man until John the Baptist, who is baptizing in the Jordan River, looks out in the crowd, points and declares, "*Behold, the Lamb of God who takes away the sin of the world!*" (John 1:29). And now, the **mystery** of the lamb is revealed and we know the personage of the Lamb; Jesus the Christ. Timing is Everything.

So, the Apostle Paul says, **Now Is The Time** to reveal the **mystery** that has been hidden in the mind of God. And the mystery he reveals is God empowered the church, bought with the blood of His Son, to share with all creation, both visible and invisible, multifaceted wisdom of God. And when God pulls back the curtain and brings the Gentiles to the forefront it is an indication that something is getting ready to happen. Watch God's timing. In verses eleven and twelve, he writes, "*This was in accordance with the eternal purpose which He carried out in Christ Jesus our Lord, in whom we have boldness and confident access through faith in Him.*"

A Family Reunion (14-21)

"For this reason I bow my knees before the Father, from whom every family in heaven and on earth derives its name, that He would grant you, according to the riches of His glory, to be strengthened with power through His Spirit in the inner man, so that Christ may dwell in your hearts through faith; and that you, being rooted and grounded in love, may be able to comprehend with all the saints what is the breadth and length and height and depth, and to know the love of Christ which surpasses knowledge, that you may be filled up to all the fullness of God. Now to Him who is able to do far more abundantly beyond all that we ask or think, according to the power that works within us, to Him be the glory in the church and in Christ Jesus to all generations forever and ever. Amen."

After helping the Gentiles appreciate, through his teachings and writings, that Jesus came and died so they could be reconciled back to God, along with the Jews in one body. The Apostle Paul wanted the Gentiles to be assured that through Jesus' death and resurrection, He removed the metaphorical signs that read, 'Jews Only,' 'Gentiles and women only,' and put up a 'Whosoever Will' sign.

The Apostle Paul has revealed the **mystery** of God, the church, the family of God on earth, and now gets on his knees and goes into prayer on behalf of the revealed **mystery**, the church. He starts in verse fourteen with the phrase, *"For this reason."* This is the same phrase used by the Apostle to start the chapter. He then introduces the spiritual relationship of heaven and earth by saying, *"from whom every family in heaven and on earth derives its name..."* This phrase concludes that all of creation, angels and fleshly beings (humans), whether in heaven or on earth, are **one** family, under the fatherhood of God.

Note: Mankind (human) in its truest existence is a spiritual being that lives in a body and is having a physical experience. But, mankind is part of the one spiritual family of God.

God is the prototype of all fatherhood. The concept of a Father is from God and not mankind. It is hard to be a good father if you do not understand the Fatherhood of God. And, the Apostle Paul says, 'he bow his knees' before a Father like God. In verse sixteen he expresses his awe that the Father would *"grant you, according to the riches of His glory, to be strengthened with power through His Spirit in the inner man..."* An interesting observation to make is in the Apostle's use of the terms 'according to' as opposed to 'out of.' The combination of the words 'according to' as it relates to God, is God's riches are unlimited. And, whatever God gives you or anyone else, it does not affect His riches, because it is 'according to.' Now, the phrase, 'out of' on the other hand, suggests that when something is given 'out of' what is available, then immediately the inventory changes because you must subtract what has been give 'out of' what is available. This is not the case with God. God gives 'according to."

In the same verse, he gives two reasons why God grants favor to His family, 'according to' the riches of His glory: to be strengthened with power; for the inner man. When the Apostle uses the word 'strengthened,' he does not get away from the concept of being powerful in Christ. In fact, he uses another form of the word 'kratos.' He uses the Greek word 'krataioo' (κραταιόω), to become strong, to prevail against and be powerful. In other words, God grants His family 'according to,' not just for them to be overcomers, but to be overcomers with 'dunamis' power. And, all of this is possible through His Holy Spirit, which lives 'in the inner man."

It is the inner man that truly needs to be strengthened. The Apostle Paul gives a detailed look at the inner man concept when he writes to the saints living in Rome. In Romans 7:18-23 he writes, *"For I know that nothing good dwells in me, that is, in my flesh; for the willing is present in me, but the doing of good is not... For I joyfully concur with the law of God in the inner man, but I see a different law in the members of my body, waging war against the law of my mind and making me a prisoner of the law of sin which is in my members."* So, the Apostle's prayer is that God grants the family 'according to' not 'out of' His riches so that the family may be strengthened through the Holy Spirit in the 'inner man.' Because, if the inner man is strengthened then the family has the ability to fight against the desires of the flesh.

This strengthened 'inner man' gives access to Christ to **"dwell in** your hearts through faith."** Christ desires to dwell (reside, inhabit, live) in your hearts, but you need to be strengthened with the power from God's Holy Spirit, that as an overcomer with power, Christ can literally be "at home," "feel welcomed," not just visit but invited to stay. And, if He stays, you will have enough strength and power to allow Him to become the **Center** of your life. The God we serve, who grants us, **not** 'out of' **but** 'according to' His riches and strengthens us through His Holy Spirit, granting Christ a home in our hearts, this same God, is able to do 'far more abundantly' than we ask or think. What is it that you need that God cannot do?

Note: If Christ is comfortable to dwell in the homes of your hearts, you cannot ask for too much. The problem is often we ask too little. The work of God is **NEVER** a money problem. It is a **FAITH** problem.

4

It's In Your Walk... (1-3)

"*Therefore I, the prisoner of the Lord, implore you to walk in a manner worthy of the calling with which you have been called, with all humility and gentleness, with patience, showing tolerance for one another in love, being diligent to preserve the unity of the Spirit in the bond of peace (Ephesians 4:1-3) – NASB.*

In the opening of what is referred to as Chapter 4, the Apostle Paul begins with the connecting word, "Therefore." It is at this juncture in his writing to the Ephesians that he transitions from the theological principles established in Chapters 1, 2, and 3, and now describes the practical applications of that theology for the believer. The remaining three chapters, the Apostle's focus is on the "**walk**" of the believer. He implores the Ephesians to "walk" in a manner worthy of the calling with which they had been called (Ephesians 4:1). His encouragement to "walk" or live a lifestyle that aligns and agrees with your spiritual calling. He begins with walking in "Unity" (Ephesians 4), walking in "Harmony" (Ephesians 5), and he closes with walking in "Victory" (Ephesians 6).

Note: Unity is not the same as uniformity. Unity comes from within and based in the spiritual. Uniformity is the result of pressure from outside and based in carnality.

To better understand the rationale in starting this section of writings with the connecting word, "Therefore," perhaps it is advantageous for us to highlight a few of the principles established in the previous chapters, so when we come to the word "Therefore," we will understand what it is There For. In Chapter 1, the Apostle Paul described how **blessed** we are as believers in Christ. He tells us "who" is blessed, "Who" is doing the blessing, the "object" of the blessings, the "magnitude" of the blessings, and "where" the blessing are located. He then highlights that all of these blessings are in Christ.

Before the believer gets distracted with how blessed and powerful they are in Christ, In Chapter 2, he says, don't be so quick to forget...

How you were once separated from God

How you were dead spiritually as a result of your trespasses and sins

How you walked according to the lusts of this world

How you served the prince of the air

How by nature you were the children of wrath

BUT GOD, being rich in mercy, made you alive in Christ through His own love and blessed you with the **gift** of salvation. Salvation is not based upon your goodness, but the goodness of God. In other words, we don't serve God "trying" to be saved, but we serve out of appreciation that we "**are**" saved. In Chapter 3, he describes why God has blessed and redeemed the believer, for it so the manifold wisdom of God might be known to the angelic hosts. The angelic hosts are those beings that existed before God created the world and these same beings wanted to understand the mystery of salvation (1 Peter 1:12). God's multifaceted wisdom is made known to all creation, both visible and invisible, by the body of Christ. And, as members of the body of Christ, part of our responsibility is to teach the angels about the manifold wisdom of God and explain the mystery of salvation. And, if that is the spiritual charge placed upon the believer by God, to teach the spiritual realm, then certainly as a child of God, there is a peculiar way we should live.

In the opening of Chapter 4, the Apostle Paul urges the believer to walk in a manner worthy of the calling with which they had been called (Ephesians 4:1). To "walk" is to live. To walk in a manner that is "worthy" means in a manner that "agrees" with your calling. The Apostle's use of the word "**worthy**" is the word-picture of equal weights or scales that are balanced. As a believer, our calling and our conduct should be in balance. In other words, the doctrine that you teach, the doctrine you believe should be seen in your conduct and evident in your life.

In verse two, the Apostle gives the believer three virtues that will assist them to walk worthy: humility, gentleness, and patience. If we are going to preserve the unity of the Spirit it is necessary that its foundation is founded in "**humility**." Humility is the opposite of pride. However, a believer should not be a promoter of false humility, but knowing their worth in Christ. Since the emphasis is on unity, perhaps the Apostle Paul lists **humility** first, recognizing pride promotes disunity, but true humility promotes unity; with Christ being the supreme example of humility (Philippians 2:6-8). In addition to humility, the believer is **gentle**. Gentleness is the opposite of being self-serving or rude. It implies that the believer has his/her emotions under control. It means you sit between two extremes: A person who is always angry and A person who is never angry. When you are "**walking**" with God you get angry at the right time for the right reason, but not at the wrong time for the wrong reason.

Note: Gentleness is not to be confused with weakness. Any two weak people can get into an argument. But, it takes a strong person to be gentle in the midst of chaos.

The third virtue that formulates unity is **patience**. Patience is a virtue of irony. It is often something we desire others to have with us, but something we seldom grant to them. However, as a believer, your culture does not get to define how **patience** will work in your life. For the believer, **patience** is the ability to endure discomfort without the need or desire to fight back. It literally means, "long-tempered." Being the possessor of all three virtues, he now tells the believer how to orchestrate a walk that is worthy, using these three virtues, that results in the unity of the Spirit. He says, *"being diligent to preserve the unity of the Spirit in the bond of peace"* (Ephesians 4:3). In other words, when you genuinely own your Christian walk with humility, gentleness, and patience, then it is a must that you become enthused to maintain and guard the unity of the Spirit. And, it is worth noting, the believer is not told to "**create**" unity, but to "**keep**" the unity that already exists in the Spirit, and it needs to be done in love.

Note: The reason there is war on the outside is there is war on the inside. If a believer cannot get along with God, he/she cannot get along with other believers.

Which One Is The One (4-6)

> *"There is one body and one Spirit, just as also you were called in hope of your calling; one Lord, one faith, one baptism, one God and Father of all who is over all and through all and in all."*

How clever of the Apostle Paul in his writings to the Ephesians.

He does not introduce spiritual unity until after he has drawn in the believer through a solid doctrinal foundation. The importance of establishing the doctrinal principles first is, when it comes to unity, the believer cannot establish true unity simply based on love and not include doctrine. So, he waited until after establishing a strong doctrinal foundation in Chapters 1, 2, and 3, and then presented the natural outflow of unity in the Spirit by naming seven spiritual currencies that "**unite**" all true believers.

Note: All biblical teachings (doctrine) have an immediate cultural context that needs to first be considered before interpreting the teachings into our current culture. And, while all believers may not agree on some matters of Christian teachings (doctrine), they do need to agree on the foundational truths of faith.

The seven spiritual traits of unity, centered on the Triune Godhead are: One **body**, One **Spirit**, One **hope** of your calling, One **Lord**, One **faith**, One **baptism**, and One **God** and Father. Now, there is one of the elements of the seven that tends to create a great deal of discussion and debate, and it is found in verse five. There is not much debate when it comes to the concept of One "**body**." This is an expression of the **body** of Christ, in which every believer is a member, through obedience by the Spirit of God. The **body** of Christ should be a direct representation of Christ in bodily form; thus, the **body** of Christ.

When it comes to discussing the One **Spirit**, there is not a great deal of disagreement regarding the Spirit. This is the same **Spirit** that indwells every believer and assists in living the Christian life. The One **hope** is the confidence that the believer should have in the promises of God, and the Spirit is the assurance of these promises. One **Lord** refers to Jesus the Christ, who died, was resurrected, and ascended to heaven for us, with the promise to reconcile His body on earth (body of Christ) with the family of God in heaven (Ephesians 3:15).

In the circles of religion, there is some talk when it comes to understanding the One **faith**. After all, faith is the belief in something to be true even when it is hard to explain. Our everyday life activities are full of things that are based on faith, yet we do not communicate them as an act of faith. For example, when you walk across the room to flip the light switch, it is you demonstrating your faith that when you flip the light switch, the wires that you cannot see, but believe are properly connected, will generate and carry enough electricity to the light bulb filament, causing the light to shine. And you did it all by faith. As it relates to the One **faith**, same concept but with a different focus. The One **faith** in the realm of Christianity is based upon the fact there is a settled foundation of truth given by Christ to His church that is agreed upon by the believers. This is referred to as the One **faith**. The Apostle Jude would later reference this One **faith** as, "that was handed down to the saints" (Jude 3).

Now, as stated earlier, the one of the seven elements that tends to create a great deal of dialogue and debate, is the sixth of the seven elements, the One **baptism**. To properly understand the contextual use of the phrase, One **baptism**, it is necessary that we spend some time understanding baptism and the different baptisms mentioned in the bible. So, before we do that, let's go ahead and address the seventh element of our spiritual unity and we will come back to do the detailed work on the One **baptism**. The seventh spiritual trait of unity is there is One **God** and Father of all who is over all and through all and in all.

On five different occasions, in this letter, the Apostle Paul compassionately refers to God as **Father** (Ephesians 1:3, 17; 2:18; 3:14; 5:20). The reference describes the relationship between God and the believer and the unity of believers with one another; being members of the family of God. And, in this family, God is Father over the family, He works through the family, and dwells within the members of the family.

Now, let's get back to the sixth of the seven spiritual traits, One **baptism**. In the realm of religion, the debate often comes when the discussion is based on the One **baptism**, because when you talk about there being One **baptism**, that includes form and authority. And, since we can read about several different baptisms in the bible, it is important when we use the phrase, "One **baptism**," we need to know, "Which One Is The One Baptism" in Ephesians 4. Baptism is an intriguing concept and by the time we are done with the topic I hope we will have a better understanding and appreciation on why baptism is essential to our salvation, and alleviate some of the confusion that may surround the concept of baptism.

One Baptism

The bible mentions at least five types of baptisms, which includes the following:

1. The baptism of John
2. The baptism of the Holy Spirit
3. The baptism of fire
4. The baptism of suffering
5. The baptism authorized by Jesus

So, when the Apostle Paul tells the Ephesian believers, "there is one baptism," in focus of these other baptisms, the question birthed out of this statement is, "Which One Is The One Baptism" mentioned in Ephesians 4? Let's look at each one in context and see if we can accurately conclude "Which One Is The One Baptism" mentioned by the Apostle.

The baptism of John

"Now in those days John the Baptist came, preaching in the wilderness of Judea, saying, repent for the kingdom of heaven is at hand. For this is the one referred to by Isaiah the prophet when he said, 'The voice of one crying in the wilderness, Make ready the way of the Lord, Make His paths straight!' Now John himself had a garment of camel's hair and a leather belt around his waist; and his food was locusts and wild honey. Then Jerusalem was going out to him, and all Judea and all the district around the Jordan; and they were being baptized by him in the Jordan River, as they confessed their sins" (Matthew 3:1-6).

The prophet John did so much baptizing in Jerusalem that he became known as John the Baptist, or a John the Baptizer. Baptist is not his name, it is his occupation.

The baptism of the Holy Spirit and Fire

This same John, the Baptist, introduces the concepts of two more baptisms to the crowd of people that were coming to be baptized; specifically, the Pharisees and Sadducees.

"As for me, I baptize you with water for repentance, but He who is coming after me is mightier than I, and I am not fit to remove His sandals; He will baptize you with the Holy Spirit and fire. His winnowing fork is in His hand, and He will thoroughly clear His threshing floor; and He will gather His wheat into the barn, but He will burn up the chaff with unquenchable fire" (Matthew 3:10-11).

The baptism of suffering

*"Then the mother of the sons of Zebedee came to Jesus with her sons, bowing down and making a request of Him. And He said to her, 'What do you wish?' She said to Him 'Command that in Your kingdom these two sons of mine may sit one on Your right and one on Your left.' But Jesus answered, '**You do not know what you are asking. Are you able to drink the cup that I am about to drink?**' They said to Him, 'We are able"* (Matthew 20:20-22).

In this passage of scripture, Jesus is standing in the shadow of the cross and He asked the two sons of Zebedee if they were willing to be baptized with the baptism of suffering that He Himself must go through. He describes to them that not many days from now He would be arrested by Roman soldiers, marched through the streets of Jerusalem, and humiliated in the presence of Pontius Pilate. His accusers would encourage the Roman soldiers to take a whip and scourge Him. Those same soldiers will take a plant of thorns, fashion it into a crown, placing it on His head as mockery of a king. Jesus explained to these two sons that He will be marched up to Golgotha's hill to be crucified between two thieves. So, the question He put before them is, "Are you able to drink of the cup that I am about drink?" Are you able to handle the baptism of suffering that I must endure? In which, foolishly they replied, "Yes."

I Have Questions...

So far, we have been introduced to the baptism of John, the Holy Spirit, fire, and suffering. So, Apostle Paul, this is a little confusing. When reading your words, "There is One **body, Spirit, hope, Lord, faith,** and **God**," there is no problem in understanding that. However, when you say, "One **baptism**" and we have read about four thus far, how are we to understand what it means to have One **baptism**? Well, if that is not enough for you, let's introduce one more baptism.

The baptism authorized by Jesus

Now, the baptism that I am about to introduce occurs after Jesus has been arrested, falsely put on trial, crucified like a criminal, buried in Joseph of Arimathea's tomb, and resurrected from the dead. And, as a resurrected Savior, Jesus had some last instructions for His holy apostles and disciples:

> *"And Jesus came up and spoke to them, saying, 'All au-*
> *thority has been given to Me in heaven and on earth. Go*
> *therefore and make disciples of all the nations, baptizing*
> *them in the name of the Father and the Son and the Holy*
> *Spirit, teaching them to observe all that I commanded you;*
> *and lo, I am with you always, even to the end of the age"*
> (Matthew 28:18-20).

There is a baptism that is done in the name or by the authority of the Father, Son, and Holy Spirit, and it is the One **baptism** authorized by Jesus.

From Five To One

To get from **Five** baptisms to the **One** baptism we need to remove four from the lists. Let's start by revisiting each baptism. When John the Baptist was baptizing, on at least one occasion he informed his followers that there is One coming after him, who is mightier than he. And John said, the One who is coming has another baptism. He is going to baptize with the Holy Spirit and fire.

When the Apostle Paul came to Ephesus, ironically, he encountered some believers who had been baptized with the baptism of John, but the Apostle introduced them into another baptism.

"It happened that while Apollos was at Corinth, Paul passed through the upper country and came to Ephesus, and found some disciples. He said to them, 'Did you receive the Holy Spirit when you believed? And they said to him, 'No, we have not even heard whether there is a Holy Spirit.' And he said, 'Into what then were you baptized?' And they said, 'Into John's baptism.' Paul said, 'John baptized with the baptism of repentance, telling the people to believe in Him who was coming after him, that is, in Jesus.' When they heard this, they were baptized in the name of the Lord Jesus" (Acts 19:1-5).

At this point in the analysis, we can conclude that the baptism of John is **not** the One **baptism** so we will remove it from the list:

1. The baptism of John
2. The baptism of the Holy Spirit
3. The baptism of fire
4. The baptism of suffering
5. The baptism authorized by Jesus

Well, that brings us to the baptism of the Holy Spirit.

"Gathering them together, He commanded them not to leave Jerusalem, but to wait for what the Father had promised, which He said, 'you heard of from Me; for John baptized with water, but you will be baptized with the Holy Spirit not many days from now'" (Acts 1:4-5).

"He said to them, 'It is not for you to know times or epochs which the Father has fixed by His own authority; but you *will receive power when the Holy Spirit has come upon you; and you shall be My witnesses both in Jerusalem, and in all Judea and Samaria, and even to the remotest part of the earth'"* (Acts 1:7).

"When the day of Pentecost had come, they were all together in one place. And suddenly there came from heaven a noise like a violent rushing wind, and it filled the whole house where they were sitting. And there appeared to them tongues as of fire distributing themselves, and they rested on each one of them. And they were all filled with the Holy Spirit and began to speak with other tongues, as the Spirit was giving them utterance" (Acts 2:1-4).

The baptism of the Holy Spirit was promised and received, so it is not the One **baptism**. And for sure, you do not want the baptism of fire or the baptism of suffering, so we will remove them from the list as well:

1. The baptism of John
2. The baptism of the Holy Spirit
3. The baptism of fire
4. The baptism of suffering
5. The baptism authorized by Jesus

So, the only baptism that is left is the baptism authorized by Jesus in His words, recorded in Matthew 28:19, and demonstrated throughout the New Testament writings. For example, consider the passage in Acts 8:25-38, with Philip the evangelist and the Ethiopian eunuch, and his request for baptism. Notice Philip's response to the request:

"So, when they had solemnly testified and spoken the word of the Lord, they started back to Jerusalem, and were

preaching the gospel to many villages of the Samaritans. But an angel of the Lord spoke to Philip saying, 'Get up and go south to the road that descends from Jerusalem to Gaza.' So, he got up and went; and there was an Ethiopian eunuch, a court official of Candace, queen of the Ethiopians, who was in charge of all her treasure; and he had come to Jerusalem to worship, and he was returning and sitting in his chariot, and was reading the prophet Isaiah. Then the Spirit said to Philip, 'Go up and join this chariot.' Philip ran up and heard him reading Isaiah the prophet, and said, 'Do you understand what you are reading?' And he said, 'Well how could I, unless someone guides me?' And he invited Philip to come up and sit with him. Now the passage of Scripture which he was reading was this: 'He was led as a sheep to slaughter; and as a lamb before its shearer is silent, so He does not open His mouth. In humiliation His judgment was taken away; who will relate His generation? For His life is removed from the earth.' The eunuch answered Philip and said, 'Please tell me, of whom does the prophet say this? Of himself or of someone else?' Then Philip opened his mouth, and beginning from this Scripture he preached Jesus to him. As they went along the road they came to some water; and the eunuch said, 'Look! Water! What prevents me from being baptized?' And Philip said, 'If you believe with all your heart, you may.' And he answered and said, 'I believe that Jesus Christ is the Son of God.' And he ordered the chariot to stop; and they both went down into the water, Philip as well as the eunuch, and he baptized him" (Acts 8:25-38).

Therefore, the One **baptism** the Apostle Paul is promoting in Ephesians 4:4 is the **one** authorized by Jesus. It is water baptism for the remission of sin, redemption by the blood of Christ, with the promise and seal of the Holy Spirit.

Gifts and Grace (7-16) 🔑

> "But to each one of us grace was given according to the measure of Christ's gift. Therefore, it says, when He ascended on high, He led captive a host of captives, and He gave gifts to men." (Now this expression, "He ascended," what does it mean except that He also had descended into the lower parts of the earth? He who descended is Himself also He who ascended far above all the heavens, so that He might fill all things). And He gave some as apostles, and some as prophets, and some as evangelists, and some as pastors and teachers, for the equipping of the saints for the work of service to the building up of the body of Christ; until we all attain to the unity of the faith, and of the knowledge of the Son of God, to a mature man, to the measure of the stature which belongs to the fullness of Christ. As a result, we are no longer to be children, tossed here and there by waves and carried about by every wind of doctrine, by the trickery of men, by craftiness in deceitful scheming; but speaking the truth in love, we are to grow up in all aspects into Him who is the head, even Christ, from whom the whole body, being fitted and held together by what every joint supplies, according to the proper working of each individual part, causes the growth of the body for the building up of itself in love.

After discussing and pleading for the unity of the Spirit amongst the believers, the Apostle now introduces a concept about the natural diversity that exists within this unified body of Christ. In verses seven and eight he states that all believers are gifted with a gift and the gift is given to us by God, the Giver. Now, the gift the Apostle Paul is referring to is different than natural abilities. When you were born into this world, the God of the universe gave you inclinations of natural abilities (art, athletics, music, etc.), and some He gave more than to others.

Note: Never take the gift and leave the Giver. The gift is the least form of expression of the Giver. The Giver is always more valuable than the gift.

In the spiritual realm, every believer has at least **one** spiritual gift, regardless of your natural abilities, you have at least one spiritual gift from God. However, the struggle sometimes, is being able to identify the spiritual gift given to you from God. And, if we cannot identify our gift, as a result, we are not properly functioning within this unified body of Christ.

The gift(s) of God are not given to us as toys to play with, but as tools for us to build up the body of Christ. And, if these tools are not used in love, they become weapons to fight with, which is what happened in the body of Christ in Corinth. This same Apostle that writes to the Ephesians writes to the Corinthians admonishing them to stop using their gifts as a means to suggest they were better than someone else (1 Corinthians 12-14). God knows what gifts to give and who to give them to. In verse seven he writes, *"But to each one of us grace was given according to the measure of Christ's gift."* In other words, God has enabled us (granted us) with the gift(s) that He is pleased to give us, and He did not give everybody the same gift. So, don't become envious of another believer's spiritual gift.

Envy of spiritual gifts will distract you and next thing you know, you're wanting to be the preacher, elder, deacon, song leader, usher, etc. When this happens, you are trying to be too much. At this point you are functioning from your **desire** as opposed to your **GIFT.**

Note: Comparison is a form of violence. When you believe you're not good enough you will compare yourself to others.

Gifts for the Gifted

In verse eleven the Apostle explains to the believers that, not only are they gifted, but God gave gifted people to the church, as a gift. *"And He gave some as apostles, and some as prophets, and some as evangelists, and some as pastors and teachers…"* In this verse, he describes four kinds of gifted people, given to the body of Christ. The first two gifts that He gives are foundational gifts to the church: Apostles and prophets. The apostles were divinely appointed ambassadors who were to give witness to the resurrection of Jesus and followers of His ministry, from His baptism of John (Acts 1:15-22). The role of the prophet in the New Testament church is slightly different than that of old. In the Old Testament, prophets were commonly associated with predicting the future of events, but in the New Testament the primary function is to be a proclaimer of the Word of God (Acts 11:27-28; Ephesians 3:5).

The latter two gifts, evangelists and pastors and teachers, are gifts that build on top of the foundational gifts. The evangelist is one who travels from place to place as a preacher or proclaimer of the Good News. Now, this last category of gifted people, "pastors and teachers," on the surface gives the impression that it is two different gifts. However, it is written in a style that is one office with two ministries.

Note: The Greek word, ποιμένας (poimenas), which is translated pastor in this verse is not a reference to the office of bishop (ἐπισκόπους; episkopous) or elder (πρεσβυτέρους ; presbyterous). The word ποιμένας (poimenas)is translated pastor and means a human leader over a community of believers, also known as the local evangelist or minister.

So, the God of the Universe has given gifted people to the body of Christ as a gift. And when you disrespect, speak against, or ignore the "gifted people" that God has given to the local church, you directly disrespect God at the same time; because they are His gifts to the body of Christ. And as members of the body of Christ, the plea of the Apostle call for unity is because each believer visibly represents the invisible. The body of Christ on earth is really an expression of God's grace.

Grace Anatomy (11-16)

Over and over, the Apostle Paul refers to the believers as "the body of Christ," but let's not become comfortable with just being the body of Christ without understanding what that really means. The body of Christ is comprised of **Container** and **Content**. The **Container** is the body, but the **Content** is the Spirit. Unfortunately, as a believer, if you become comfortable with simply being the body of Christ, you are just a **Container** with no **Content**, and you become ignorant of your purpose in this Spirit-filled body.

Note: Ignorance is a learned behavior. Because we are inquisitive by nature, you have to be trained to be ignorant.

The word "anatomy" is defined as the art of separating the parts of an organism in order to ascertain their position, relations, structure, and function. So, when I reference the body of Christ as God's Grace Anatomy, I am suggesting what God expects from this body is a result of how it has been **Formed**, **Filled**, and designed to **Function**. This process of Formed, Filled, and Function can be traced throughout God's creation. Consider the creation account in Genesis 1, *"In the beginning God created the heavens and the earth, and the earth was formless and void"* (Genesis 1:1-2). A few highlights surrounding

God's creation process. On day one He created natural lights. Day two He created the sky and the seas. Day three He created dry land. Day four He created the sun and the moon. Day five He created the birds and the fish. Day six He created living creatures on the ground. Everything He had created from Days one to six, He created it by speaking it into existence.

However, when He got ready to make man, God does not speak to man, He **forms** him. Man is the first thing in creation that God **touches**. Everything else He stood back from it and spoke it into being (Let there be…) and it became. But, He touched man and we have been needing His touch ever since.

God **formed** man from the dust of the earth. Now, what He formed was not the **content**, it was the **container**. He **formed** the container and then breathed into him the "content," the breath of life. This is a demonstration of God **filling** up what He has **formed**. And as the body of Christ, the Apostle Paul wants us to see that God will always **fill** what He **forms**. Even looking back at the six days of creation, He formed the sky and filled it with birds. He formed the seas and filled it with fish. He formed man and filled him with breath. God **forms**, **fills**, and expects it to **function**.

The God of the Universe speaks through the Apostle Paul, to the body of Christ in Ephesus, telling them, "I **Formed** you, I **Filled** you, and now you must **Function**. Unity in the body of Christ is the manifestation of the properly **functioning**. An important observation from God is, 'you cannot function just because I formed you. I must fill you.' The body of Christ only functions in unity when it is filled with the Spirit. All of God's creation functions according to the filling.

Note: Everything God has formed, He also filled. And if it's filled it should function. If there is a place where unity does not exist, it is because what has been "formed" has been "filled" with a contrary spirit.

Even in your personal life's journey, you will go through a stage in life where God is metaphorically, forming you. And, you will perhaps begin to ask questions of God on what it is happening to you and why so many changes? In which God responds, 'It is happening because I have you on the wheel and I am forming (shaping) you, so I can take you into the "filling" stage of life.' And, when God gets through forming and filling you, His expectation is for you to function.

When you look throughout the New Testament, you will see the body of Christ **functioning**, whether it is one person, 25, 300, or 3000. And the challenge, for us as the body of Christ today is, if there is no difference in the filling then there should be no difference in our functioning. Every member in the body has a function. The body works better when the members function. This is even true in the human body. The body works better when the kidneys, lungs, pancreas, tonsils, eyes, legs, etc., function.

The Apostle Paul brings closure to his plea for unity for the body of Christ by analogizing it with the human body. He writes, *"from whom the whole body, being fitted and held together by what every joint supplies, according to the proper working of each individual part, causes the growth of the body for the building up of itself in love"* (Ephesians 4:16). In the human body, the illustration is God sends the supply of what the body needs at the connection point of every joint. Break the connection and you will lose the supply. Lose the supply and you miss the blessing.

Note: To Function in unity as a body it requires us to interact with people, crucify our feelings, pride, and thoughts, and stretch to make the connection at the joint.

The mystery of how to function as the body of Christ in unity is found in our own fleshly body. For example, if you cut your knee, your body will immediately start the process to fix the cut. Your body will send white blood cells to the area to ward off infection. And, while that is occurring your skin cells will begin to stich the skin back together. While the stitching is in process, a scab will form to cover you until the stitching is complete.

Now, if your own fleshly body will do that, why can't the spiritual body of Christ do that when somebody gets injured in the body? It is not necessary for the body to kill them, but what if we metaphorically sent spiritual white blood cells to the spot of injury, start the process of stitching them back together, and cover them with a spiritual scab of protection, until they are healed (Galatians 6:1). It is truly a mystery of the body of Christ. He formed us, He filled us, and now He expects us to function in unity, as a body. And not just a body, but the **body of Christ.**

5

Walk This Way... (1-8)

"Therefore be imitators of God, as beloved children; and walk in love, just as Christ also loved you and gave Himself up for us, an offering and a sacrifice to God as a fragrant aroma" (Ephesians 5:1-2) – NASB.

The challenge in verses one and two is for us to walk in love "as" Christ also have loved us. If it was just for us to walk in love and it did not say "as" Christ has also loved us, then it would not be so challenging. But the challenge is to get your walk to be a reflection of what Christ did with you. The Apostle Paul uses this basic concept throughout his writings. The Apostle Paul encourages the believer to imitate outwardly what Christ has done with you inwardly. What is that exactly? Learning to treat people the way Christ has treated you. Therefore, if we do not learn to walk in the way that Christ has commanded us to walk, then our life becomes a "lie." And, we have lied about who He is by the way we handle other people.

So, the Apostle Paul is challenging us now to do as Christ has done and reminds us that it is a sacrifice. And the sacrifice is a fragrant aroma (sweet smelling savor).

Note: Nobody becomes a fragrant aroma (sweet smelling savor) in the nostrils of God without sacrifice.

A sacrificial life for the believer requires that you put your "will" on the cross, nail what you would say to the cross, and allow your fragrant aroma, the burning of your flesh, to become an incense in the nostrils of God. God receives the glory every time you restrain what you would "say" and "do" and give up on you, to reflect Him. That is where the incense comes from. Anything else stinks in the nostrils of God.

Verses 3-4

"But immorality or any impurity or greed must not even be named among you, as is proper among saints; and there must be no filthiness and silly talk, or coarse jesting, which are not fitting, but rather giving of thanks"- NASB.

He continues to focus on the walk of the believer and the moral issues with a group of believers whose morality has not been legislated by their conversion. Appreciate the idea that there is a misnomer that once a person is converted their morality towards the world's system just naturally dissipates. That is simply not the case. Yes, there are some people who are able to adjust more quickly in their morality than others, however, if you are left "untaught," you can give your whole heart to Jesus and still find yourself engaged in immoral behavior and not discern the line of distinction. That is why Christian character and morale has to be taught. These basic principles are considered the milk of the Word. They are foundational trues. They address your character, morality, and your disposition. And from there, the believer should leave the first principles of the doctrine and move into the principles of maturity, so the believer can learn to walk in love, the same way Christ has loved us.

Verses 5-10

"For this you know with certainty, that no immoral or impure person or covetous man, who is an idolater, has an inheritance in the kingdom of Christ and God. Let no one deceive you with empty words, for because of these things the wrath of God comes upon the sons of disobedience. Therefore do not be partakers with them; for you were formerly darkness, but now you are Light in the Lord; walk as children of Light (for the fruit of the Light consists in all goodness and righteousness and truth), trying to learn what is pleasing to the Lord" (Ephesians 5:5-10) – NASB.

One of the joys in reading the book of Ephesians is we get to witness the skilled Apostle Paul use his abilities to address the different cultures, background, mindsets, and the current racial divisions amongst the believers and balance them through their relationship in Jesus. For example, one moment he is talking to the Jews and the people who are steep in tradition and have great faith, but he challenges them not to be arrogant. Then, there are times when he is talking to the Gentiles and heathens, who came from orgies and idolatrous backgrounds, and encourages them to let go of those idols. Then, he will turn back to the Jews and remind them, that it is not about keeping feasts, and to the group at large he encourages them to love one another. He is trying to bring all sides of the believers together, which is a picture of the church today. The church is not just one group of people, but many walks of life that have come together in Christ, and now have to learn to walk in Christ, as one.

Note: You can be light and not walk in Light. Learn to walk like who you are and not what you come from.

The Apostle Paul explains the relationship with Light should correspond in the behavior of the believer. Since they are children of Light, that is, since their very nature is spiritual light, they are to live accordingly. In verse nine there is a parenthetical explanation that the fruit of the Light—which is goodness, righteousness, and truth, reflects God's character in the life of the believer. The fruit of the Lord, is the Spirit of God, coming together with the spirit of man, producing the offspring of God's character in you. This is the after effects of the intimate relationship that develops between the spirit of the believer and God's Spirit, as we live in this earth realm of our existence. The evidence that you have been with God, is the fruit of the Lord in your life, which is your testimony that you have been with God.

Choosing A Life of Consistency (15-21)

"Therefore be careful how you walk, not as unwise men but as wise, making the most of your time, because the days are evil. So then do not be foolish, but understand what the will of the Lord is. And do not get drunk with wine, for that is dissipation, but be filled with the Spirit, speaking to one another in psalms and hymns and spiritual songs, singing and making melody with your heart to the Lord; always giving thanks for all things in the name of our Lord Jesus Christ to God, even the Father; and be subject to one another in the fear of Christ" (Ephesians 5:15-21) – NASB.

In these next few verses, the Apostle Paul explains to the believer how to be properly filled by expressing what you "**can't**" have and comparing it to what you "**can**" have. The essence is, instead of being intoxicated with wine, be intoxicated with the Holy Spirit. There are many parallels between wine and the Holy Spirit, but I will only introduce a couple. The readers of the Apostle Paul's letter were familiar with the process of making wine. In their day it was not unusual to walk down the street and see someone stomping on the grapes and pressing out the wine. And, they knew the bursting of the grape produced the wine, and the fermenting process caused the wine to rise up in the cup, for they saw this happen all the time. However, what the Apostle Paul is trying to get them to appreciate is Christ "**was**" that grape, and through Him being wounded for our transgressions and bruised for our iniquities (Isaiah 53:5), is how the Holy Spirit comes to us. Thus, we are commanded to drink and be filled with the Holy Spirit.

Now, it does not matter what a person's theological background is when trying to understand the men in the upper room in Acts chapter 2, but what we do know is those men could not have been real conservative. You may be wondering, 'why would I say that?' Because, no one would have walked into a room and seen people sitting in silence and still and conclude, *"they are full of sweet wine"* (Acts 2:13). Unfortunately, many believers have been led to believe that the experience in the upper room occurred in a boardroom, Americanized type structure, amongst a group of intellectuals, with their shirts and ties, looking important, who just so happen to have the Holy Spirit.

Observational Note. The narrative in Acts 2 about the upper room, gives the impression that the people in that room were high spirited and highly expressive in their experience. To use an Americanized colloquialism, *they were cutting up pretty bad*. One, they were cutting so bad, the noise was down in the streets. It was the noise that got the attention of the people. So, the noise coming from the room attracted the people from the street and once the people got up to the room and saw the people in the room, it was then that the people from the street concluded, *"these men are full of sweet wine,"* since they had never seen men totally under the influence of anything, other than liquor. The crowd was correct in that these men were under the influence of something. But it was the influence of the Holy Spirit.

The Apostle Paul is explaining how the Holy Spirit has the ability to influence you and he compares it to the influence of wine in the human system. For example, wine is an external substance that is taken internally. It gets in the belly and affects the entire body. In the same sense, if the Holy Spirit be in you, your body is going to be affected by the presence of the Holy Spirit. Affected in such a way that it is "outwardly" obvious there has been an internal ingestion of the Holy Spirit. Your sight is affected, your reactions are affected, your judgment is affected, your thinking is affected, because of what you have been drinking. And, the Apostle Paul says, 'that is the way I want you to be in the Holy Spirit.' He commanded the believer to be filled with the Spirit.

Note: It is not by your bumper sticker on your car that the world should know you have the Holy Spirit. It is through your behavior which should demonstrate that you are under **divine control**.

In verse 19, he begins to tell them "how" to be filled with the Spirit. *"speaking to one another in psalms and hymns and spiritual songs, singing and making melody with your heart to the Lord."* You have to be intimate with God. Perhaps people spend too much time speaking to people and not enough time speaking to the Lord. Singing hymns and making melody in your heart. God wants you to come into His presence without an agenda, and just come and worship Him. This is a level of intimacy with God that causes you to become intoxicated with your relationship with Him. Now, keep in mind that the Apostle Paul is defining the **mystery** of the church.

So, as much as possible, divorce your mind from the idea of what you have been "taught" church is supposed to be, and think about the fact the early church did not act, move, or behave, the way the church acts, move, and behave today. Let's go back to the blueprint in the scripture and see that the early church walked around in a **power** that would embarrass most believers today. The early church walked around, murmuring to themselves, in psalms, hymns, spiritual songs; making up songs to the Lord and creating melody in their hearts to the Lord. This is personal, private, and intimate.

A Prearranged Marriage (22-33)

"Wives, be subject to your own husbands, as to the Lord. For the husband is the head of the wife, as Christ also is the head of the church, He Himself being the Savior of the body. But as the church is subject to Christ, so also the wives ought to be to their husbands in everything. Husbands, loves your wives, just as Christ also loved the church and gave Himself up for her, so that He might sanctify her, having cleansed her by the washing of water with the word, that He might present to Himself the church in all her glory, having no spot or wrinkle or any such thing; but that she would be holy and blameless. So husbands ought also to love their own wives as their own bodies. He who loves his own wife loves himself; for no one ever hated his own flesh, but nourishes and cherishes it, just as Christ also does the church, because we are members of His body. For this reason a man shall leave his father and mother and shall be joined to his wife, and the two shall become one flesh. This mystery is great; but I am speaking with reference to Christ and the church. Nevertheless, each individual among you also is to love his own wife even as himself, and the wife must see to it that she respects her husband" (Ephesians 5:22-33) – NASB.

In these verses, God reveals His plan for marriage for the couple, before He reveals His plan for the church. In reality, God's plan for the couple is in its essence a **picture** of His plan for the church. What

God reveals about Adam and Eve, the man and his wife, is just an illustration of what the church will ultimately be to Him. In the midst of this dissertation of scripture, the Apostle Paul explains how the wife should submit to her husband and how the husband should love his wife. But, all of this makes sense when we properly understand verse 32, when he pens, *"This mystery is great; but I am speaking with references to Christ and the church."*

The Apostle Paul, from verse 22 through verse 31, goes through the details of marriage and the husband and wife relationship, only to get to verse 32 to make the point that he is not really talking about marriage, but used it as the illustration to get to the **mystery** of Christ and the church. To truly appreciate this **mystery** of Christ and the church and its connection to husband and wife, we have to go back to discuss the first man, Adam.

The first man, Adam, was created in the likeness and image of God. The One God, who was ready to create a picture of Himself in the earth, created "one" man, Adam. Male and female, He created them and called their name, "Adam." The first man, Adam, did not look like any man that came after him. Adam was unique in his creation, which is one of the things that separates him from all men, born of a woman. Adam was created, not born. And since he was not born, he did not have an umbilical cord connecting him to a mother. He never experienced childhood, for God created him full grown. And, uniquely, when God created him, He also created the woman at the same time. Observe this principle. When the One God was ready to bring forth the woman, He did not go back to the ground to create the woman, but went inside the man and pulled out of him what was already in him; a woman.

Note: The "fe" in female is the contraction for fetus. The female is the male that carries the fetus. The "wo" in woman is the contraction for womb. The woman is the man that has a womb.

However, before God went inside of the man and pulled out of him, the woman, the one man, Adam, walked around for a period of time alone. **Observational note.** The word "alone" is comprised of two words, "all" and "one." The "al" is the contraction for the word "all" and the "alone" literally means, "all-one." The one man Adam is "all-one." He is "alone." Now, we do not know how long he was alone, but it was long enough for all the animals to be brought before him and named. And, at the end of naming all the living things, there was not a suitable mate for him. This is the first time that God looks at His creation and said, "It is not good for man to be alone"; all-one. That is the first time you will read in Genesis where God said something was not good.

So, God takes Adam, lays him down and puts him in a deep sleep. This is the first anesthesia experience. God says to Adam, 'I will not have to reach back to the dirt to create anything for you. Because you are so much like Me, that you are all sufficient, that I just have to reach inside of you and pull out of you what is already in you.' And it was out of his side, God pulled the woman. And when Adam woke from his anesthesia, he looked and saw the woman and said, 'She is me. She is my body. She is bone of my bone, flesh of my flesh. She is just like me, but with a womb. She is my body.' And the two becomes one, because they were one, **before**.

Note: This is the **mystery** of the church. We were His **before**.

As a result of both, man and woman, eating the forbidden fruit, the bible says, 'the woman was deceived, but not the man.' Adam was not deceived when he ate the fruit. It was his decision that cost the fall to all humanity. The woman was deceived but the man decided. Out of his decision to die with his bride, chaos broke out in the kingdom and everything under their domain went down with them. It is important to know, the word 'kingdom' means the 'kings domain.' Therefore, if the king falls everything under him falls too.

Consider this thought, as it pertains to God, there has only been two men created. The first man Adam, and the last man Adam. And, everybody else was "born" in them. In Galatians 4:4, it records, "*But when the fullness of the time came, God sent forth His Son, born of a woman, born under the Law.*" This Son, that is called Jesus, is the second man, Adam. He comes again. Complete in Himself. Born of a virgin without an earthly father. And, since He had no earthly father, there is no earthly blood, meaning there is no contamination in His blood. So, now we see a **new creation** potential, because we have blood that has not been tainted in the fall of Adam. Hence, He becomes the second Adam.

The second man, Adam, in His three years of ministry goes to His own people, to the Jews and His own do not receive Him (John 1:11), suggesting there is no suitable mate found for Him. But the same Father that said to the first Adam, "I AM going to bring something out of you, said to the second Adam, 'If You will go to the cross,' in which the second Adam responds, 'If I have to go through this in order to get Me a wife, then drive the nails in my hands and my feet, and pierce Me in the side.'

Observe the powerful parallels between the first and second Adam. While the first Adam lay sleeping, the Father reached inside of him and pulled out his bride. The second man, Adam, while He lay on the cross, a Roman soldier pierced Him in His side, and when His side was opened, out came blood and water, and it was in His blood that brought for the church, which is His bride. **Observational note.** The first man, Adam, said, 'If my wife is going to die, then I am going to die with her.' But, the second man, Adam, said, 'Since My wife is dead, I AM going to die for her.' And, since He is innocent of her sin, He is eligible to die in her place and redeem her from her sin. **This is** **the mystery of the church**. It was this attraction that made Him go to the cross.

Note: The cross is Jesus giving His body to His bride.

The love affair between Jesus and the church is seen when the church looks at Jesus and says, 'He is my savior, He is my deliverer, and He is my husband.' This is one of the rationales on the interchangeable text, where Jesus will call the church His bride and then later refer to her as His body. If it challenges you to think of the church as His body and His bride, then recall the first marriage between the first man and woman, which was his bride and his body. **This is the mystery of the church**. When the Apostle Paul begins to reveal the **mystery**, he refers to the church as the body of Christ and then he calls the church the bride of Christ, and he is correct in both.

In verses 22 through 33, marriage is not the topic or the issue. Marriage is the **illustration**. The issue is the **mystery** of Christ and the church, but he illustrates the **mystery** on earth through the marriage. And, he challenges the believers to make their marriage a sacrifice to Him, so people who cannot see the **mystery** can see your marriage, and perhaps seeing your marriage, may understand the **mystery** of Christ and the church. To illustrate this principle, both, the man and the woman are deeply challenged, because the woman has to play the role of the church. She has to submit. And, the man has to love her, like Christ loves the church. And, for this to work you will have to crucify your flesh.

> *"For this reason a man shall leave his father and mother and shall be joined to his wife, and the two shall become one flesh. This mystery is great; but I am speaking with reference to Christ and the church. Nevertheless, each individual among you also is to love his own wife even as himself, and the wife must see to it that she respects her husband"* (Ephesians 5:31-33) – NASB.

6

Relationship "Over" Regulations (1-9)

"Children, obey your parents in the Lord, for this is right. Honor your father and mother (which is the first command-ment with a promise), so that it may be well with you, and that you may live long on the earth. Fathers, do not provoke your children to anger, but bring them up in the discipline and instruction of the Lord. Slaves, be obedient to those who are your masters according to the flesh, with fear and trembling, in the sincerity of your heart, as to Christ; not by way of eyeservice, as men-pleasers, but as slaves of Christ, doing the will of God from the heart. With good will render service, as to the Lord, and not to men, knowing that what-ever good thing each one does, this he will receive back from the Lord, whether slave or free. And masters, do the same things to them, and give up threatening, knowing that both their Master and yours is in heaven, and there is no partiality with Him" (Ephesians 6:1-9) – NASB.

In 1950, the University of Michigan conducted a "one question" survey, led by Dr. Jawanza Kunjufu, to identify the number one influence on the character of children. Here are the top five responses from the 1950 survey:

1950 Survey Results

1. Home
2. School
3. Church
4. Peers
5. Television

In 1950, the home was the number one influence on the character of children. Thirty years later, the same survey with the same question was conducted, yet it yielded different results. The top five responses from the 1980 survey:

1980 Survey Results

1. Home
2. Peers
3. Television
4. School
5. Church

The home was still the number one influence on the character of children, however, the school dropped to number four, peers moved up to number two, and the church went from number three to last place. Ten years later, the University conducted the same survey, and again, different results. Here are the top five responses from the 1990 survey:

1990 Survey Results

1. Television
2. Peers
3. Home
4. School
5. Church didn't make the list

Notice the drastic change on the number one thing that was shaping the mind of children in 1990, was Television; moving from third place ten years prior to number one. The home dropped from number one to third place and the church did not make the list at all. Ten years later, it is the same survey, conducted by the same University, led by the same professor, and again, there are different results. Listed below are the results from the year 2000 survey:

2000 Survey Results

1. Television
2. Peers
3. Internet
4. Church
5. Home didn't make the list

This survey, conducted by the University of Michigan, has identified some of the major challenges that affect the spiritual and physical health of the home. In the 2000 survey, television was still the number one influencer on the character of children. And, a new influencer made the list called the Internet. The Internet replaced the home for third place, and the home did not make the top five list of influencers on the character of children in the year 2000.

Note: Be careful what you allow to feed you. Because, what feeds you will lead you.

The Apostle Paul opens this final chapter to the Ephesian believers by speaking directly to the children. He did not ask the parents to speak to or admonish them, he, the Apostle writes directly to the children. So, when this letter is read to the Ephesian believers, with the children in attendance of the reading, they too would hear their role in bringing spiritual health to the body of Christ. In verse one he writes, *"Children, obey your parents in the Lord, for this is right"* (Ephesians 6:1 – NASB). The harmony in the home is based on everybody in that home.

Harmony in the home is a form of worship to God. For example, when the wife submits to her husband "as unto the Lord" this is a form of worship. When the husband loves his wife "as Christ loves the church" this is a form of worship. When children obey their parents "in the Lord" this too is a form of worship. And, when everybody functions according to their role, there is harmony in the home.

Teaching With God (2-4)

"Honor your father and mother (which is the first commandment with a promise), so that it may be well with you, and that you may live long on the earth. Fathers, do not provoke your children to anger, but bring them up in the discipline and instruction of the Lord."

The concept of honoring your father and mother surpasses the idea of simply obeying them. The word "honor" manifests the emotional behavior of respect, love, and valuing the life of your parents and emotionally and physically caring for them as long as they need you. Bringing honor to your parents was also evident in the way you lived. However, when a father and/or mother have not provided an environment that requires obedience, those children will be exposed to a heart of rebellion, which could possibly shorten their life on this earth (Ephesians 6:3).

Note: Parents should not discipline their children based on the social cliché, "Do as I say, not as I do." Children **hear** what you do LOUDER than what you actually **say**.

It is a truism that children want to know the limits. Children prefer structure over chaos. But, if they are not taught, through word and example, parents could be preparing their children for a collision course with rebellion. And, the bible is full of examples where parents neglected their children, either through a bad example or failing to provide discipline to their children. For example, King David pampered Absalom, giving him a bad example, and the results for Absalom were tragic. Eli failed to discipline his sons, resulting in disgrace to his name and the nation of Israel.

In verse four, the Apostle Paul writes, "*Fathers, do not provoke your children to anger, but bring them up in the discipline and instruction of the Lord.*" The fathers are addressed because they represent the governmental head of the family, given by God. And, the responsibility rests upon the governmental head to make sure there is a healthy disciplinarian environment for the children. God placed that responsibility on the **father**. In order to create an environment that encourages growth for the children, the Apostle Paul says, "Fathers, do not provoke your children to anger..." Translation, do not exasperate your children with **unreasonable demands**, petty rules out of selfishness, showing favoritism, breaking promises, and demeaning their character by the way you talk to them.

A father that will purposely provoke his child to anger is a father who is willing to behave as a child and through a **tantrum** in order to get his way. Tantrums are dysfunctional forms of trying to control other people. For observational purposes, there are at least three types of tantrums: Physical, Verbal, and Emotional.

Physical tantrums are expressed in your behavior and could result in you breaking things, throwing objects, falling on the floor, due to unresolved anger that exists in your adult life. It is unrealistic for a parent to expect their child not to behave through physical tantrums when that is the example they see from their parents.

Note: You cannot give your child outwardly what you do not have inwardly. It is hard to speak peace "outwardly" when there is no peace "inwardly."

Verbal tantrums are not centered around using foul language or screaming at the top of your voice; although they can contribute to the tantrum. However, verbal tantrums are based in the things that you **know** would hurt a person if you were to say them, and you say them to purposely injure them. Verbal tantrums strip people of their dignity, pride, and self-respect. Verbal tantrums are analogous to a person who shares their heart with you during a moment of transparency and vulnerability, and out of anger, you used what they shared with you against them.

Emotional tantrums are the manifestations of emotional lock down. In other words, it is the result of not communicating your frustrations, which could ultimately lead to **emotional abandonment.** Emotional tantrums are different than Physical and Verbal tantrums. Perhaps you didn't beat them (physical), or use injurious language (verbal), but emotionally denied them, because of unresolved anger. God states that anybody that can become angry and stay angry is a fool. In Ecclesiastes 7:9, it reads, "*Do not be eager in your heart to be angry, for anger resides in the bosom of fools.*"

Fathers are not afforded the opportunity to have Physical, Verbal, and/or Emotional tantrums before their children, if they desire to please God and avoid provoking their children to a point of anger. The father is the **point-man** in the family and God has given him the responsibility to create an environment in the home that provides, physical, verbal, emotional, and spiritual growth in the Lord. When parents are able to set a healthy teaching environment in the home, it will insulate the children from many of the things the school or society will try to teach them. For when conflict arise, the children will recall what father and mother taught them, and choose healthy teaching over distractions.

For example, when Moses was born and became the adopted son of the daughter of Pharaoh, Moses' mother was hired to be his nurse. She also became his first teacher and taught him about Yahweh, the God of Israel. Although Moses was raised as an Egyptian and educated in Egyptian schools, learning about Ra (sun god), Hathor (god of the earth), Osiris (god of death), Isis (god of magic), and Amun (god of creation), when Moses became a man, he had to make a choice. He had to decide if he was going to embrace what his mother taught or the schools. And the writer of the book of Hebrews records, *"By faith Moses, when he had grown up, refused to be called the son of Pharaoh's daughter, choosing rather to endure ill-treatment with the people of God than to enjoy the passing pleasures of sin, considering the reproach of Christ greater riches than the treasures of Egypt; for he was looking to the reward"* (Hebrews 11:24-26) – NASB.

The Armor of God and Spiritual Warfare (10-17)

"Finally, be strong in the Lord and in the strength of His might. Put on the full armor of God, so that you will be able to stand firm against the schemes of the devil. For our struggle is not against flesh and blood, but against the rulers, against the powers, against the world forces of this darkness,

against the spiritual forces of wickedness in the heavenly places. Therefore, take up the full armor of God, so that you will be able to resist in the evil day, and having done everything, to stand firm. Stand firm therefore, having girded your loins with truth, and having put on the breastplate of righteousness, and having shod your feet with the prepara- tion of the gospel of peace; in addition to all, taking up the shield of faith with which you will be able to extinguish all the flaming arrows of the evil one. And take the helmet of salvation, and the sword of the Spirit, which is the word of God."

There is another world that we seem to be oblivious to and perhaps do not take too seriously, and that is the spiritual world. Although it is less appealing to our natural senses, it is a world that is more real than the physical world that we are currently inhabitants. However, if you truly consider our makeup, mankind is a **spiritual** being. You are not your **body**. We are **souls**, made alive with the **spirit**, and we live in a body. We are spiritual beings, wrapped in flesh and having a physical experience. And, most of the trouble that you will experience has its roots in your "**soulish**" man. That is, in your thoughts, emotions, and will. If it were not for those constant reminders of our past days, we would have nothing to wrestle with.

The Apostle Paul undeniably declares that we are all in a fight and this fight is not physical. He writes, *"For our struggle is not against flesh and blood, but against the rulers, against the powers, against the world forces of this darkness, against the spiritual forces of wicked- ness in the heavenly places"* (Ephesians 6:12) – NASB. As a spiritual being, having a physical experience, your mind is trapped between the physical and the spiritual and each force is trying to dominate the other. The reality is all of us are wrestling with something; physical and spiritual. The concern is, we have spent a lot of time preparing ourselves to fight physical battles, but the Apostle Paul tells us, we are not wrestling against flesh and blood, but against rulers, powers, world forces of darkness, and spiritual forces of wickedness in the heavenly places.

The Apostle's reference to rulers, powers, world forces, and spiritual forces of wickedness is **not** a reference to people or physical things, but to ranks of angels and demons. Now, to properly understand the Apostle Paul's usage of these terms it is vitally important to understand what the New Testament writers believed about spiritual warfare, its origin, and their worldview of its impact on their life. In order to do that, we need to take a journey to the Old Testament and review some scripture, with the intent of understanding it the way the original writers purposed it and the original audience embraced it. Once we have gained Old Testament understanding of spiritual warfare, we will then come back and make the connection to the Apostle Paul's reference to spiritual warfare in the heavenly places.

Note: It would be dishonest of us to claim that the biblical writers read and understood the text the way we do as modern readers, or intended meanings that conform to theological systems created centuries after the text was written. **Our context is not their context**. Seeing the bible through the eyes of an ancient reader requires shedding the filters of our traditions and presumptions. They processed life in supernatural terms.

When it comes to supernatural transgression, there is a narrative that is not discussed much in Sunday sermons or bible studies, but it had a great impact on the spread of wickedness on the earth. This can be found in Genesis 6:1-5, where the story references the sons of God fathering their own earthly children known as Nephilim. Genesis 6:1-5, reads, "Now it came about, when men began to multiply on the face of the land, and daughters were born to them, that the sons of God saw that the daughters of men were beautiful; and they took wives for themselves, whomever they chose. Then the Lord said, 'My Spirit shall not strive with man forever, because he also is flesh; nevertheless his days shall be one hundred and twenty years. The Nephilim were on the earth in those days, and also afterward, when the sons of God came in to the daughters of men, and they bore children to them. Those were the mighty men who were of old, men of renown. Then the Lord saw that the wickedness of man was great on the earth, and that every intent of the thoughts of his heart was only evil continually."

The bible does not say a whole lot in Genesis about what happened, however, fragments of this narrative appear elsewhere in the bible, the Jewish bible, Jewish traditions, and the Septuagint, the Greek translation of the Jewish bible, which the New Testament authors knew well and even quoted them in their writings. For example, when the Apostle Peter writes, "For if God did not spare angels when they sinned, but cast them into hell and committed them to pits of darkness, reserved for judgment; and did not spare the ancient world, but preserved Noah, a preacher of righteousness, with seven others, when He brought a flood upon the world of the ungodly; and if He condemned the cities of Sodom and Gomorrah to destruction by reducing them to ashes, having made them an example to those who would live ungodly lives thereafter;" and when the Apostle Jude writes, "Now I desire to remind you, though you know all things once for all, that the Lord, after saving a people out of the land of Egypt, subsequently destroyed those who did not believe. And angels who did not keep their own domain, but abandoned their proper abode, He has kept in eternal bonds under darkness for the judgment of the great day...", both Peter and Jude are quoting a well-known Jewish book called 1 Enoch.

The book of 1 Enoch was popular with Jews of Jesus' day and with Christians in the early church. The Apostles Peter and Jude thought enough of the book that they included it in their letters. In the book of 1 Enoch, it speculates that the sons of God, which are angelic beings, wanted to help humanity by giving them divine knowledge, and then became distracted and began mating with the daughters of men. The book of 1 Enoch also gives explanation for where **demons** come from. Demons are the disembodied spirits of dead Nephilim that were killed before and during the flood. And now, as disembodied spirits, the demons roam the earth harassing mankind and seeking re-embodiment.

Note: The descendants of the Nephilim of Genesis 6:1-5 are called Anakim and Rephaim (Numbers 13:32-33; Deuteronomy 2:10-11). Some of the Rephaim are in the underworld realm of the dead with the Serpent (Isaiah 14:9-11).

Here is an excerpt from the book of 1 Enoch, the group of passages that both, Apostles Peter and Jude quote in their writing. This excerpt is taken from **The Lexham English Septuagint** (Enoch 6:1-8; 7:1-6).

1 Enoch 6:1-8

And it happened that when the sons of men multiplied in those days, they begat good and beautiful daughters. And the angels, the sons of heaven, saw them and longed for them and said to one another, "Come let us choose for ourselves women from among the people and bring forth for ourselves children." And Semiaza, who was their ruler, said to them, "I fear you may not wish to do this deed and I alone will be responsible for a great failure." Therefore they all answered him, "Let us all swear by an oath, and devote one another to mutual destruction, not to turn back from this decision until we complete it and do this deed." Then they all made a vow together and put each other under a curse in regard to this. These are the names of their rulers: Semiaza (this was their ruler of all the angels), Arathak, Kimbra, Sammane, Daniel, Arearos, Semiel, Iomiel, Chochariel, Ezekiel, Batriel, Sathiel, Atriel, Tamiel, Barakiel, Ananthna, Thoniel, Rhamiel, Aseal, Rhakiel, Touriel. These are the chiefs of tens among them.

I Enoch 7:1-6

Then they took for themselves women, each of them choosing a woman for themselves. They began to go to them and defile them. And they taught them sorcery and enchantments and cutting of roots and explained herbs to them. But those who became pregnant, brought forth great giants from three thousand cubits. These giants ate up the produce of the men. When the men were not able to provide for them, the giants had courage against them and ate up the men. And they began to sin against birds and wild animals and reptiles and fish, and each one of them ate up the flesh and drank the blood. Then the earth brought up charges against the lawless ones.

Note: The prophetic curse on the Serpent and the divine transgression that followed are the early stages to what the Apostle Paul calls **spiritual warfare**—the battle between good and evil. It is a war fought on battlegrounds in two realms: the seen and the unseen.

Consider this. If you are under attack right now, it is not a physical thing that is attacking you. Now, it may come through a physical manifestation or a physical person, but there is a **spirit** that is after you. You are fighting against a **spirit**. And, if you don't learn some techniques in spiritual warfare and what the Apostle Paul is teaching, you are going to be overtaken by situations that you are supposed to take over. But if you are fighting in your flesh, that means the enemy is killing you in your spirit, and we have to learn how to proper **arm** ourselves with the **armor of God** to obtain the victory.

Keep in mind the words of the Apostle Paul, "For our struggle is not against flesh and blood, but against rulers, against powers…" His reference to **rulers** and **powers** is not physical and earthly dominion, but the angelic host. **Rulers** and **Powers** are two ranks of angels, who are considered as fallen angels. To see a more detailed reference of the ranks of angels, see Chapter Three of this book. In addition to the fallen angels, there is the activity of demons, disembodied spirits. Demons are cursed to wonder, seeking dry places, looking for un-inhabited places, a body, that they can possess to exercise all of their cravings.

Note: You are under surveillance all the time. It does not matter how spiritual you are, disembodied spirits are always watching you, wanting to possess your body to control you. Every act that you do is motivated by a spiritual force. Who is controlling you when you do what you do? What spirit is being satisfied through your body?

An Exorcism In Progress

In Mark 5, verses 1 – 20, Jesus is directly involved with what the Apostle Paul describes as "spiritual wickedness in the heavenly places," and it is fallen angels **and** disembodied spirits. In this particular narrative, we know that the man is demonically possessed and he is possessed by a multitude of demons referred to as Legion. In New Testament times the standard size of the legion was 6000. This man in Gerasenes has a multitude of disembodied spirits that possess his body. This man has lost his sociological status and he is living amongst the tombs.

What is interesting in this narrative is when Jesus and His disciples arrive on banks of Gerasenes, the man possessed with Legion, the disembodied spirits, comes running toward Him. On the surface, it looks like two spiritual forces have come to a designated spot to fight this spiritual battle. How, the demonic possessed man runs to Jesus and falls on his knees, pleading with Jesus not to **torment** him, and not force him to leave the region.

Note: Principalities work in geographical regions. Certain spirits work in certain areas. Certain spirits work on certain families.

What is intriguing about this narrative is when Jesus and the demon possessed man meet, the demons do not resist Jesus, but pleads not to be tortured. One theological question comes to mind and that is, "How did Legion know Jesus was coming?" Perhaps, the submission of demons to Jesus is based on the spiritual fight He had earlier with the fallen angels. In Mark 4, beginning at verse 35, Jesus makes the statement, "*Let us go over to the other side.*" When they left for sail, the waters were calm, but a hurricane came out of nowhere and formed on the Sea of Galilee. Here is a note of observation. It is natural for a hurricane to appear in the ocean, but what is a hurricane doing in the middle of a lake. A lake is too small for a storm that big. This is not a natural storm.

Note: This hurricane is a form of spiritual warfare, fallen angels who have taken the form of a physical storm, attempting to stop Jesus from reaching Legions.

This storm occurred during the time Jesus was asleep on the boat and it brought great fear to the disciples, that they awoke Jesus to save them. Observe Jesus' response to the storm, which is really an active session of spiritual warfare. In Mark 4 verse 39, it says, "And He got up and rebuked the wind and said to the sea, "Hush, be still." And the wind died down and it became perfectly calm." The phrasing in this verse is important, in order to properly understand the spiritual fight on the waters. Jesus did not command the winds, but He **rebuked** the wind. So, after Jesus defeats the fallen angels in spiritual warfare on the waters, when He arrives to Gerasenes in Mark 5, the demons, aware of the defeat of the fallen angels on the water, the demons, called Legion, fell down and worshipped Him.

Note: When the bible uses the word "**rebuke**" it is always against a spirit. The thing you are fighting in your life is not a hurricane. It is a **spirit**. Don't reason with it. **Rebuke** it.

So, take the narratives from Genesis 6, 1 Enoch 6-7, and Mark 4-5, and properly make application of their interpretations and now you have a clear understanding what was on the Apostle Paul's mind and his worldview towards the supernatural, when he writes in Ephesians 6:12, "For our struggle is not against flesh and blood, but against the rulers, against the powers, against the world forces of this darkness, against the spiritual forces of wickedness in the heavenly places."

The Armor of God (13-17)

Spiritual warfare is real. You cannot fight this war through your flesh. You only win this battle by fighting it in your spirit, but you have to be properly clothed in the right armor. The detailed description of the **armor** may have resulted from the Apostle Paul being tied to a Roman soldier during his imprisonment, awaiting trial (Acts 28:16, 20). He outlines six elements that properly protects the believer from the schemes spiritual wickedness:

1. The girdle of truth
2. The breastplate of righteousness
3. The shoes of the gospel
4. The shield of faith
5. The helmet of salvation
6. The sword of the Spirit

Since we are fighting against rulers, powers, world forces of darkness, and spiritual forces of wickedness, in heavenly places, we need special equipment. God has provided the "**whole armor**," because He knows Satan and his fallen army looks for the unguarded areas of your life. If the believer puts on the **girdle of truth** it will hold the other parts of the armor together. Truth is the element of the armor that allows a person of integrity to stand with a clear conscience before the enemy without fear. The **breastplate of righteousness**, covered the body from the neck to the waist, both front and back. It symbolizes our protection in Christ. The life we live as a believer will either fortify us against the enemy or make it easier for him to attack us. The **shoes of the gospel** allows the believer to be able to stand and withstand, while taking the gospel of peace with us, wherever we go. The **shield of faith** protects the believer from the spears, arrows, and darts of the enemy. A Roman soldiers shield was so large that if the solders interlocked shields they could march into battle like a solid wall. As the believer is armed with the **shield of faith**, this suggests the believer is not in the battle alone and if we interlock with one another, we can walk **by faith**, while trusting in the promises of God.

The **helmet of salvation** is the metaphor for a mind that is controlled and protected by God. Since Satan desires to attack the mind, it is imperative that believers put on the **helmet of salvation**. The helmet allows the believer to be taught the truth, grow in grace, and protected from the craftiness of Satan's conversation. The **sword of the Spirit** is the believer's offensive weapon. A physical sword requires the hand of the soldier, but the **sword of the Spirit** has its own power, for it is "living and powerful" (Hebrews 4:12). The irony between a physical and spiritual sword. A physical sword wounds to injure and kill, while the **sword of the Spirit** wounds to heal and give life.

Note: The "whole armor of God" is a picture of Jesus. He is the Truth, He is Righteousness, He is Peace, He makes possible our faith, He is our salvation, and He is the Word of God. When you trust in Jesus, you receive the armor.

The Benediction (18-24)

"With all prayer and petition pray at all times in the Spirit, and with this in view, be on the alert with all perseverance and petition for all the saints, and pray on my behalf, that utterance may be given to me in the opening of my mouth, to make known with boldness the mystery of the gospel, for which I am an ambassador in chains; that in proclaiming it I may speak boldly, as I ought to speak. But that you also may know about my circumstances, how I am doing, Tychicus, the beloved brother and faithful minister in the Lord, will make everything known to you. I have sent him to you for this very purpose, so that you may know about us, and that he may comfort your hearts. Peace be to the brethren, and love with faith, from God the Father and the Lord Jesus Christ. Grace be with all those who love our Lord Jesus Christ with incorruptible love.

Prayer is the power source that enables the believer to fight this spiritual battle and properly wear the armor of God. You cannot fight a spiritual battle based on your own strength, no matter how strong you are. Consider the between Israel and Amalek in Exodus 17:8-

16. During the battle, Moses went to the mountaintop to **pray**, while Joshua used the sword to fight in the valley. It took both, **prayer** and the sword to gain the victory. But, not just any kind of prayer. The Apostle Paul encourages the believer to pray always, but do not only pray to ask God for things, yet get involved in intercession, supplication, and prayers of thanksgiving. Prayers of thanksgiving are great weapons in defeating the enemy. Intercession for others can also bring victory in your life. And these prayers are to be done **in the Spirit**, not from selfish motives to satisfy your flesh. **This is a spiritual warfare**.

When the Apostle Paul closes his letter to the Ephesians, he reminds them that we are not fighting this battle alone. There are other believers who stand with us in this battle, and we should encourage one another. He was so thankful for the encouragement that he received from his fellow worker, Tychicus, that he sent him to Ephesus to do for them what he had done for the Apostle. What a true encouragement it is to be a part of the family of God. Nowhere in the New Testament do we find an **isolated** believer. Believers are comparable to sheep; they flock together. The body of Christ is an army and as soldiers we need to stand together and fight together. No matter what our circumstances may be, in Jesus Christ we are "**blessed with every spiritual blessing in the heavenly places in Christ**."

Bibliography

Barclay M. Newman Jr., _A Concise Greek-English Dictionary of the New Testament._ (Stuttgart, Germany: Deutsche Bibelgesellschaft; United Bible Societies, 1993).

Charles Caldwell Ryrie, _Basic Theology: A Popular Systematic Guide to Understanding Biblical Truth_ (Chicago, IL: Moody Press, 1999).

Chŏng-hun Kim, _The Significance of Clothing Imagery in the Pauline Corpus_, vol. 268, Journal for the Study of the New Testament Supplement (London; New York: T&T Clark International, 2004).

D. E. Aune, _"Archon,"_ ed. Karel van der Toorn, Bob Becking, and Pieter W. van der Horst, _Dictionary of Deities and Demons in the Bible_ (Leiden; Boston; Köln; Grand Rapids, MI; Cambridge: Brill; Eerdmans, 1999).

David H. Stern, _Jewish New Testament Commentary : A Companion Volume to the Jewish New Testament_, electronic ed. (Clarksville: Jewish New Testament Publications, 1996).

David Martyn Lloyd-Jones, _The Christian Warfare: An Exposition of Ephesians 6:10–13_ (Edinburgh; Carlisle, PA: Banner of Truth Trust, 1976).

Eberhard Nestle et al., *The Greek New Testament*, 27th ed. (Stuttgart: Deutsche Bibelgesellschaft, 1993).

F. F. Bruce, *The Canon of Scripture (Downers Grove, IL: Inter-Varsity Press, 1988)*.
Faithlife Study Bible (Bellingham, WA: Lexham Press, 2012, 2016), Eph 1:1–2.
Glenn Graham, *An Exegetical Summary of Ephesians*, 2nd ed. (Dallas, TX: SIL International, 2008).

J. I. Packer, *Concise Theology: A Guide to Historic Christian Beliefs* (Wheaton, IL: Tyndale House, 1993).

Johan Lust, Erik Eynikel, and Katrin Hauspie, *A Greek-English Lexicon of the Septuagint : Revised Edition* (Deutsche Bibelgesellschaft: Stuttgart, 2003).

Johannes P. Louw and Eugene Albert Nida, *Greek-English Lexicon of the New Testament: Based on Semantic Domains* (New York: United Bible Societies, 1996).

Ken Penner and Michael S. Heiser, *"Old Testament Greek Pseudepigrapha with Morphology : Alternate Texts"* (Bellingham, WA: Logos Bible Software, 2008).

Marvin Richardson Vincent, *Word Studies in the New Testament*, vol. 3 (New York: Charles Scribner's Sons, 1887).

Max Zerwick and Mary Grosvenor, *A Grammatical Analysis of the Greek New Testament* (Rome: Biblical Institute Press, 1974).

Michael S. Heiser, *Supernatural: What the Bible Teaches about the*

Unseen World—And Why It Matters, ed. David Lambert (Bellingham, WA: Lexham Press, 2015).

New American Standard Bible: 1995 Update (La Habra, CA: The Lockman Foundation, 1995).
R. H. Charles and W. O. E. Oesterley, *The Book of Enoch* (London: Society for Promoting Christian Knowledge, 1917).
Rick Brannan et al., eds., *The Lexham English Septuagint* (Bellingham, WA: Lexham Press, 2012).

Robert Duncan Culver, *Systematic Theology: Biblical and Historical* (Ross-shire, UK: Mentor, 2005).

The Bible Knowledge Commentary: An Exposition of the Scriptures, ed. J. F. Walvoord and R. B. Zuck, vol. 2 (Wheaton, IL: Victor Books, 1985).

The Lexham Analytical Lexicon of the Septuagint (Bellingham, WA: Lexham Press, 2012).

The Lexham English Septuagint (Bellingham, WA: Lexham Press, 2012).

The New Testament in the Original Greek: Byzantine Textform 2005, with Morphology. (Bellingham, WA: Logos Bible Software, 2006).

Timothy Friberg, Barbara Friberg, and Neva F. Miller, *Analytical Lexicon of the Greek New Testament*, Baker's Greek New Testament Library (Grand Rapids, MI: Baker Books, 2000).

Warren W. Wiersbe, *The Bible Exposition Commentary*, vol. 2 (Wheaton, IL: Victor Books, 1996).

Warren W. Wiersbe, _Wiersbe's Expository Outlines on the New Testament_ (Wheaton, IL: Victor Books, 1992).

William Arndt et al., _A Greek-English Lexicon of the New Testament and Other Early Christian Literature_ (Chicago: University of Chicago Press, 2000).

CPSIA information can be obtained
at www.ICGtesting.com
Printed in the USA
BVHW030224140621
609519BV00006B/210

9 781478 798743